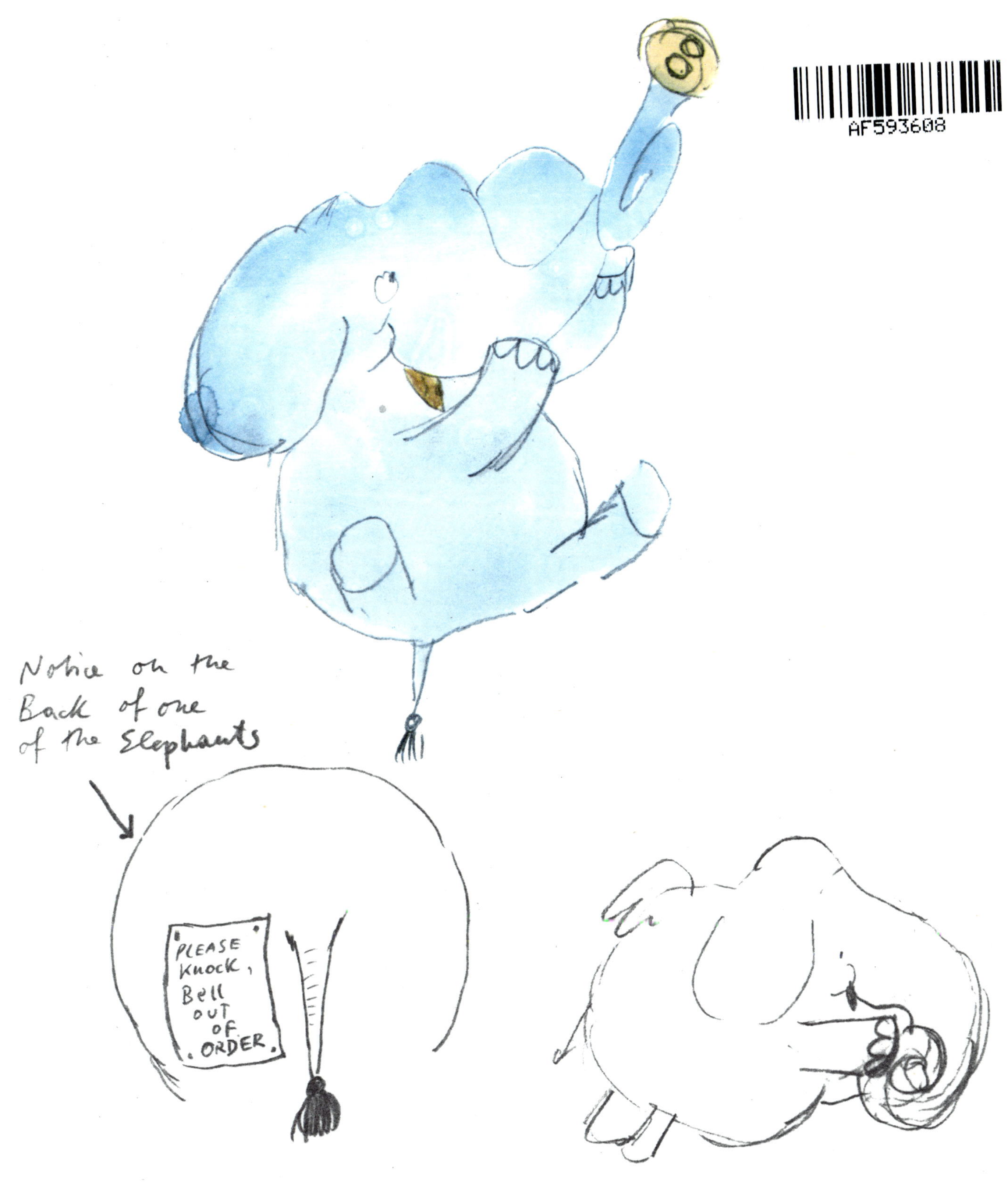
Notice on the
Back of one
of the Elephants
PLEASE
KNOCK,
Bell
OUT
OF
ORDER
AF593608

HOFFNUNG'S ENCORE

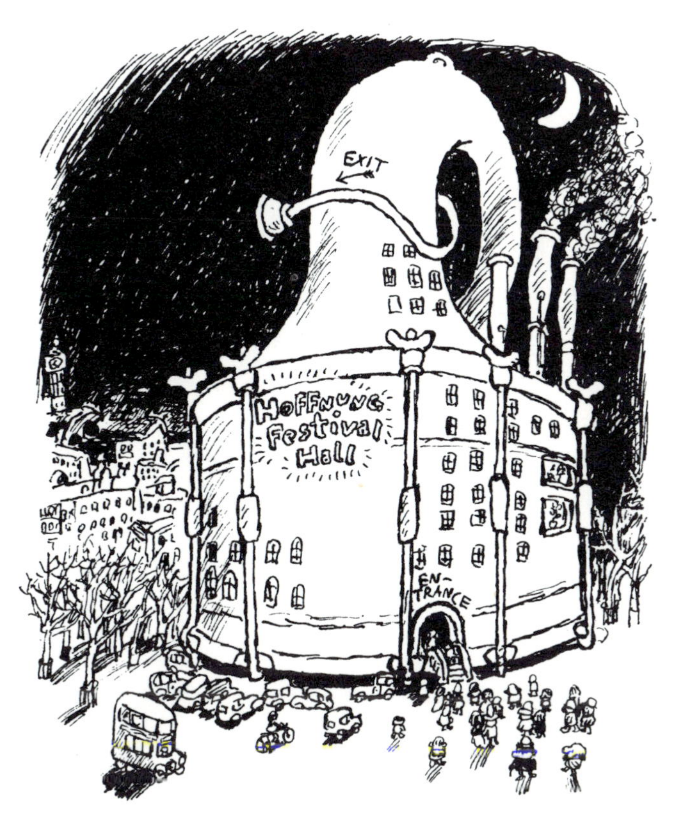

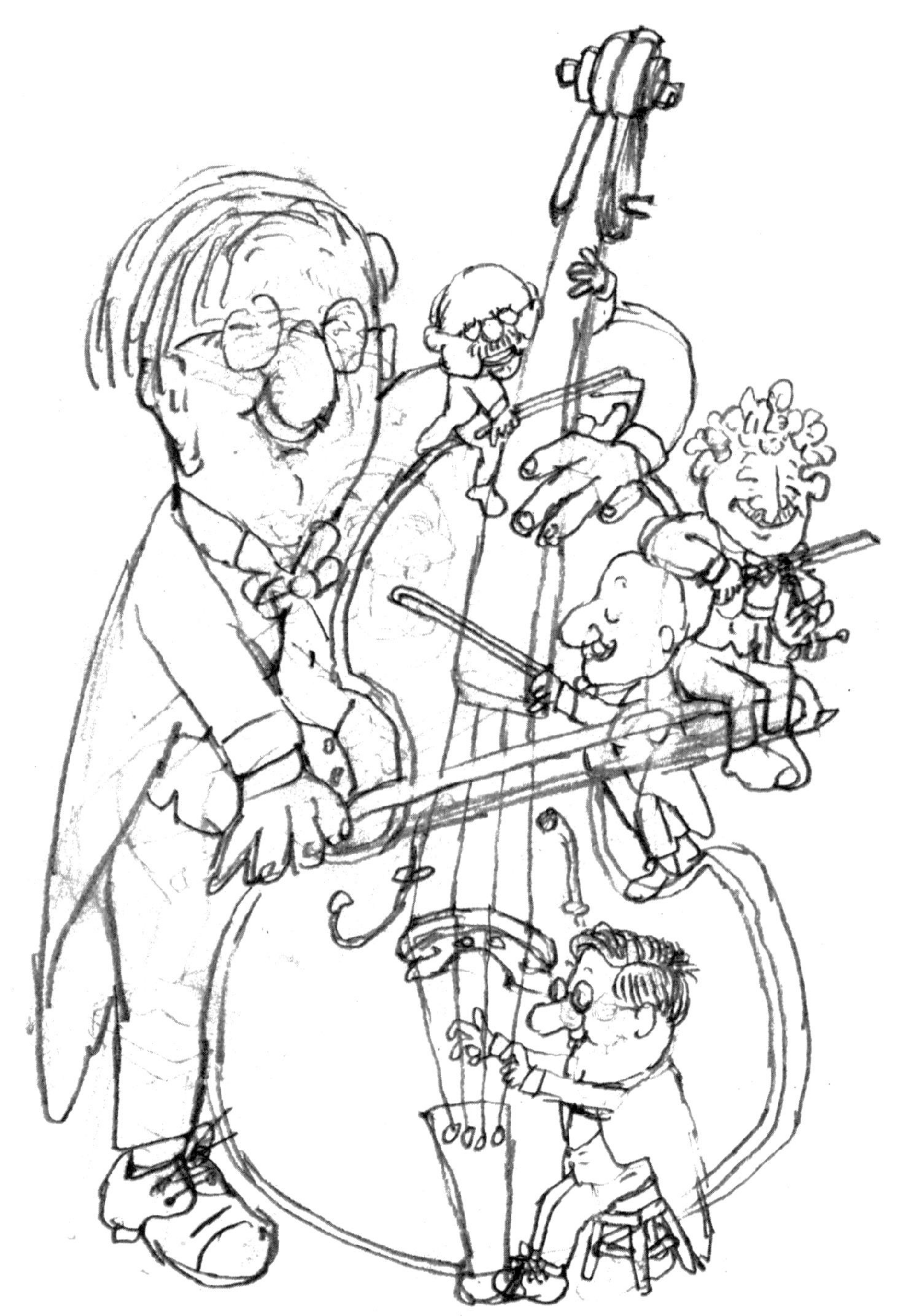

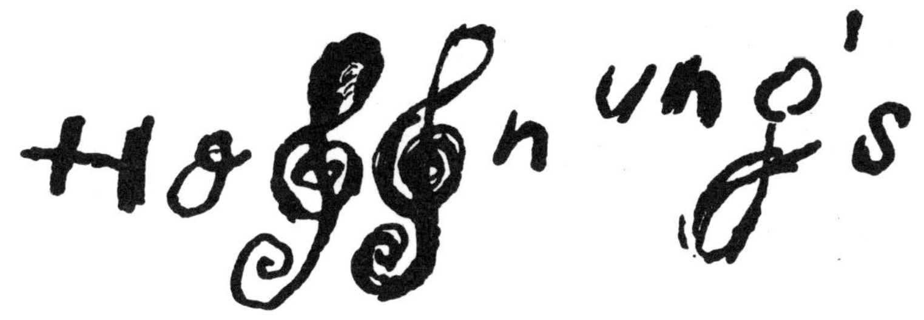

ENCORE

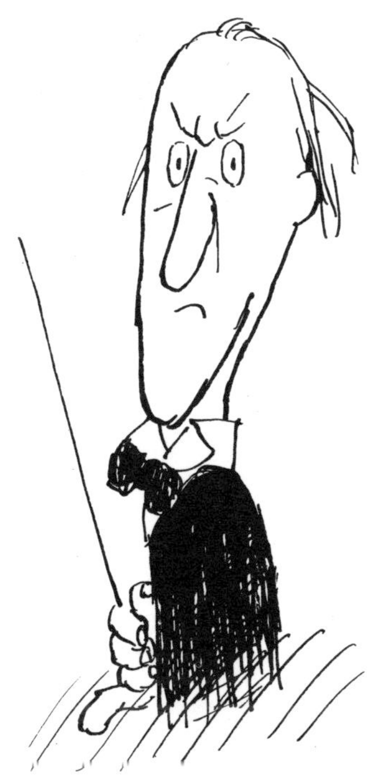

LONDON : DENNIS DOBSON

For Benedict and Emily

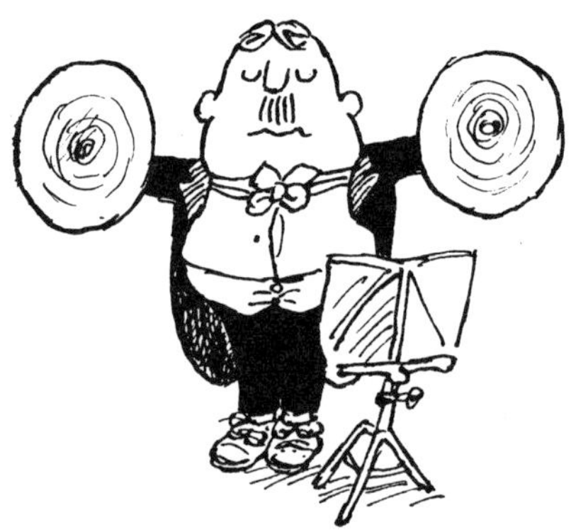

Annetta Hoffnung is grateful to the five friends who have allowed their original Hoffnung drawings to be reproduced in this book.

Thanks are also due to the proprietors of *Punch* and the management of Glyndebourne Festival Opera.

First published in Great Britain in 1968
by Dobson Books Ltd, 80 Kensington Church Street, London W8
Reproduced and printed by Colour Reproductions Ltd, Billericay
SBN 234 77248 4

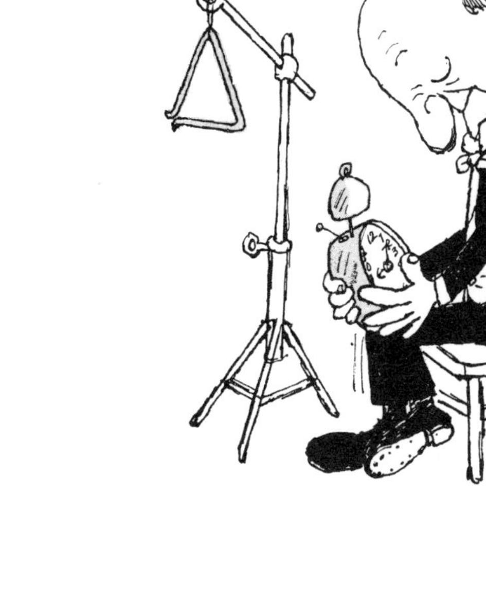

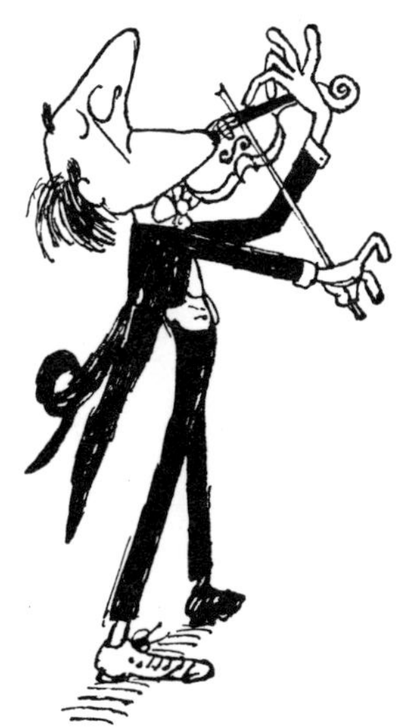

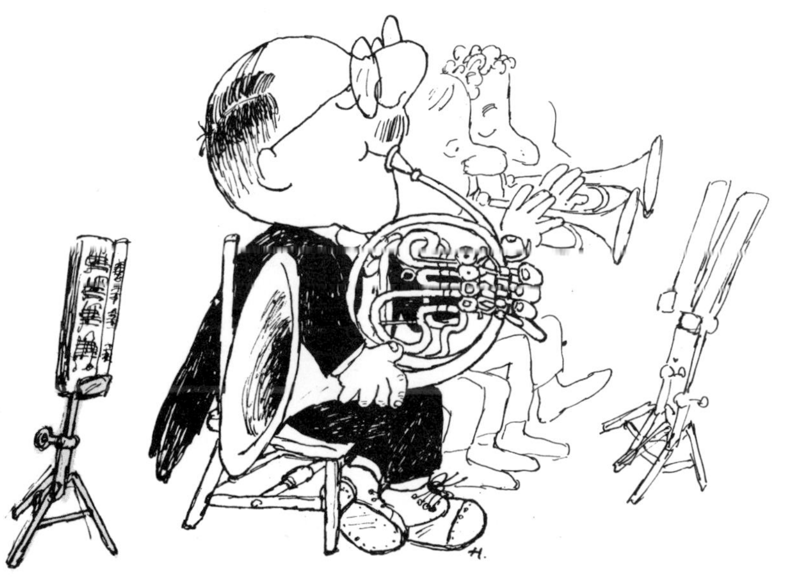

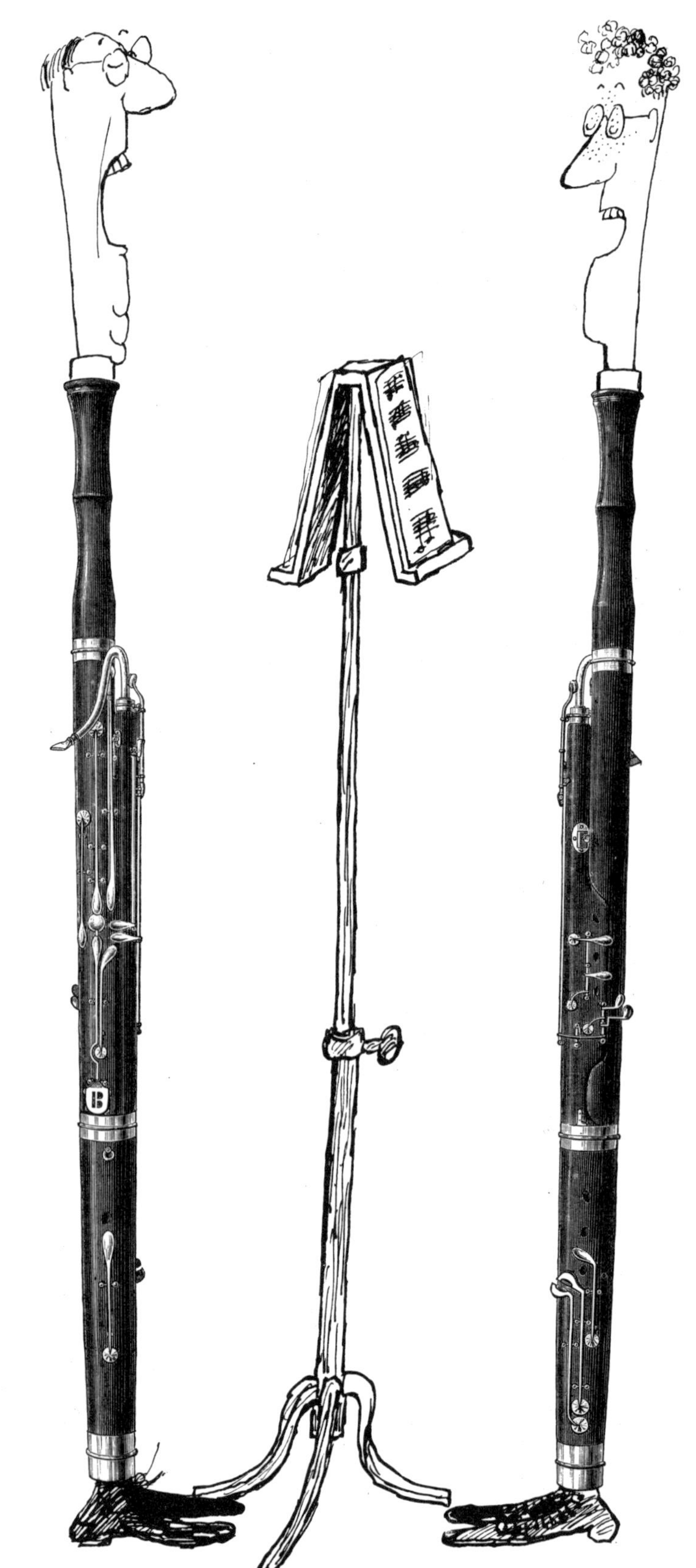

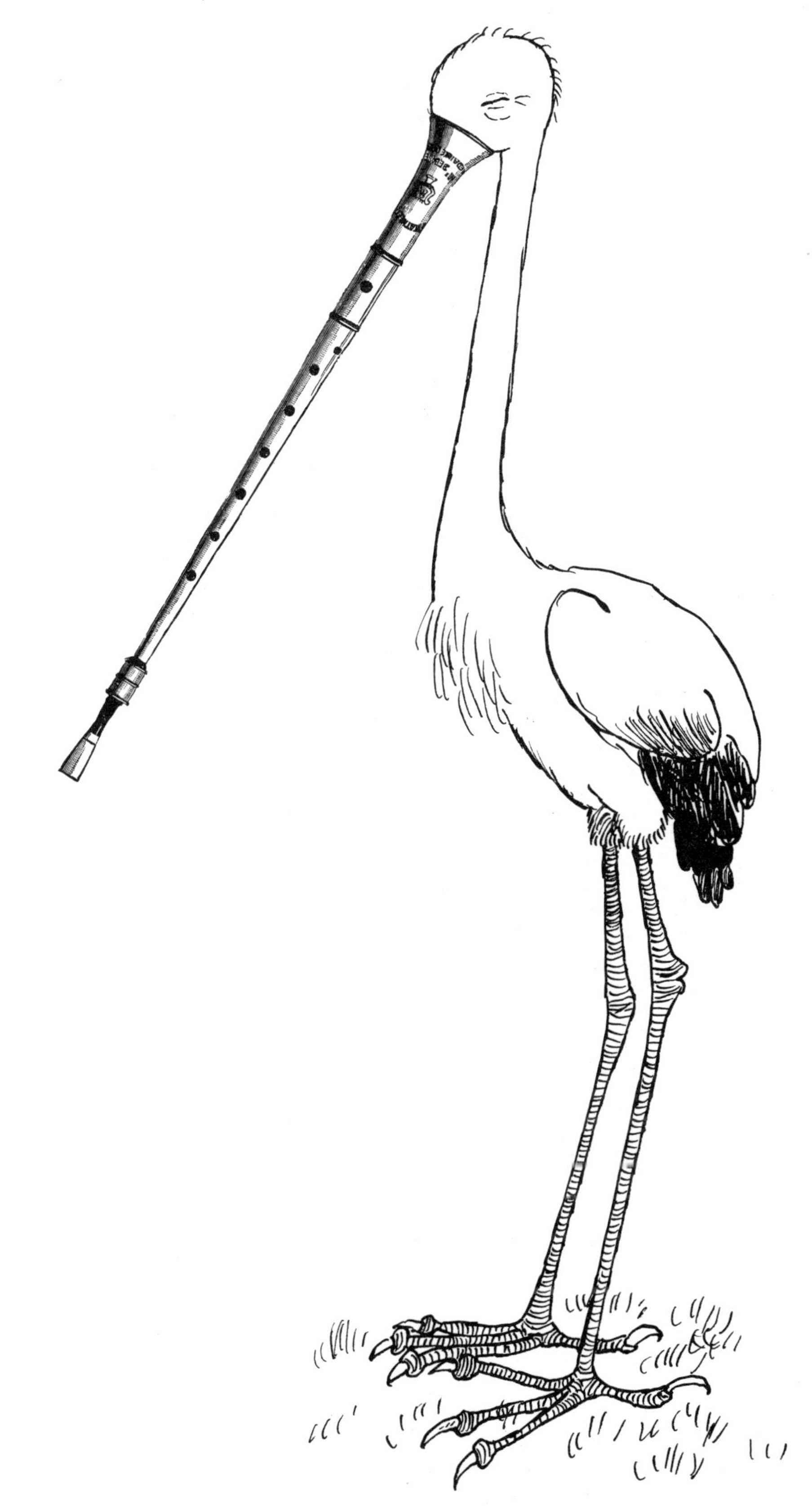

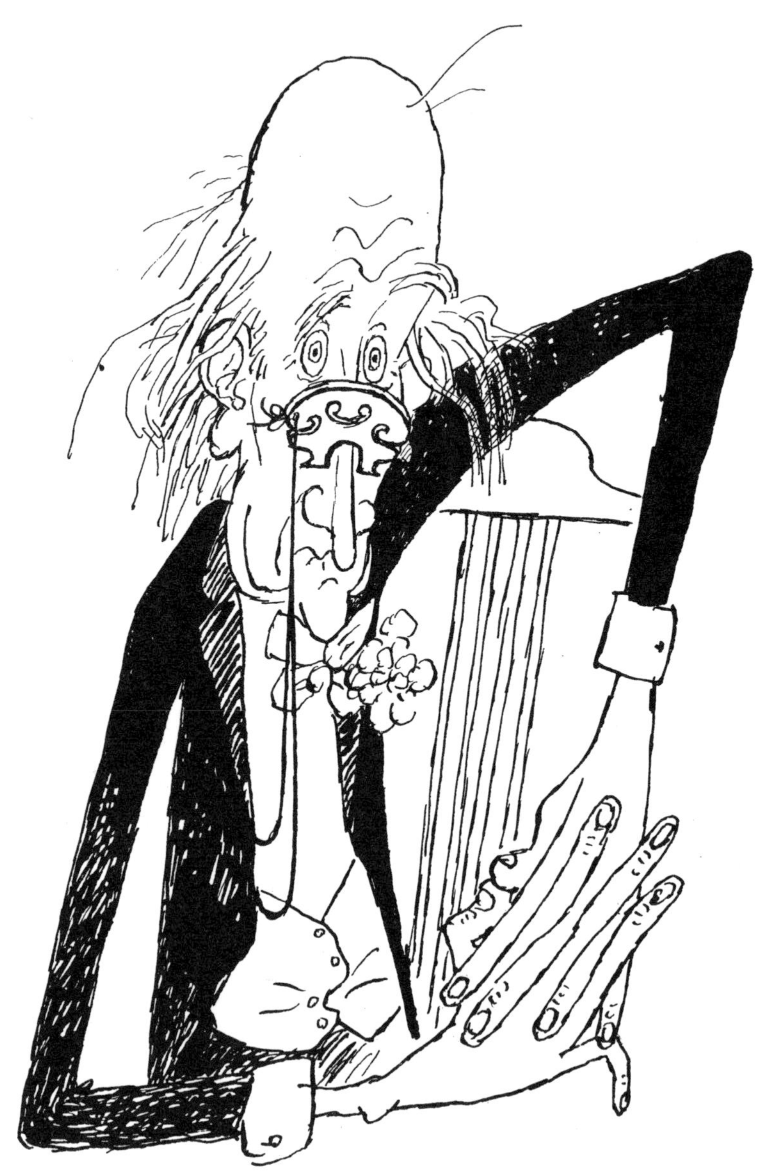

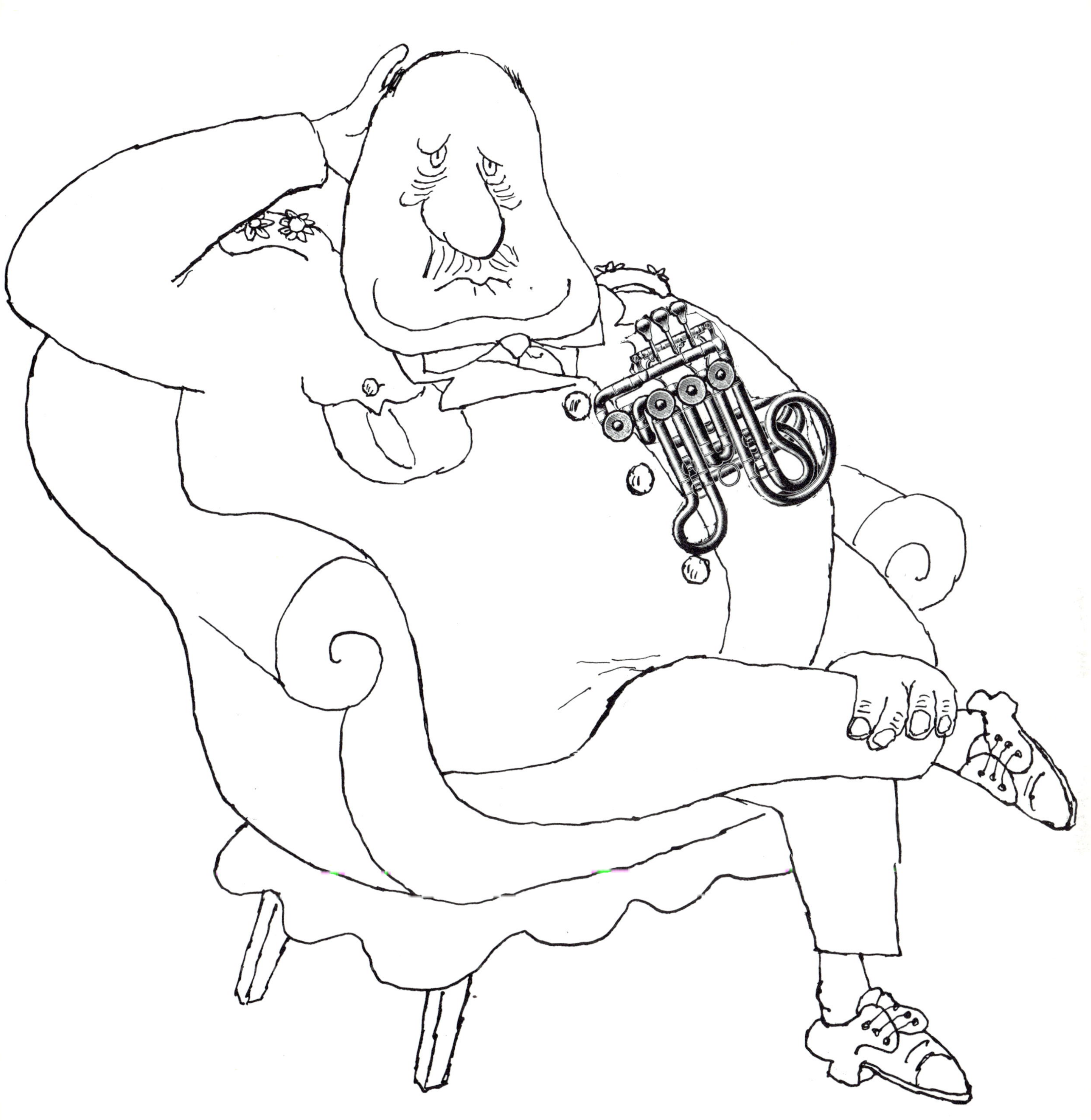

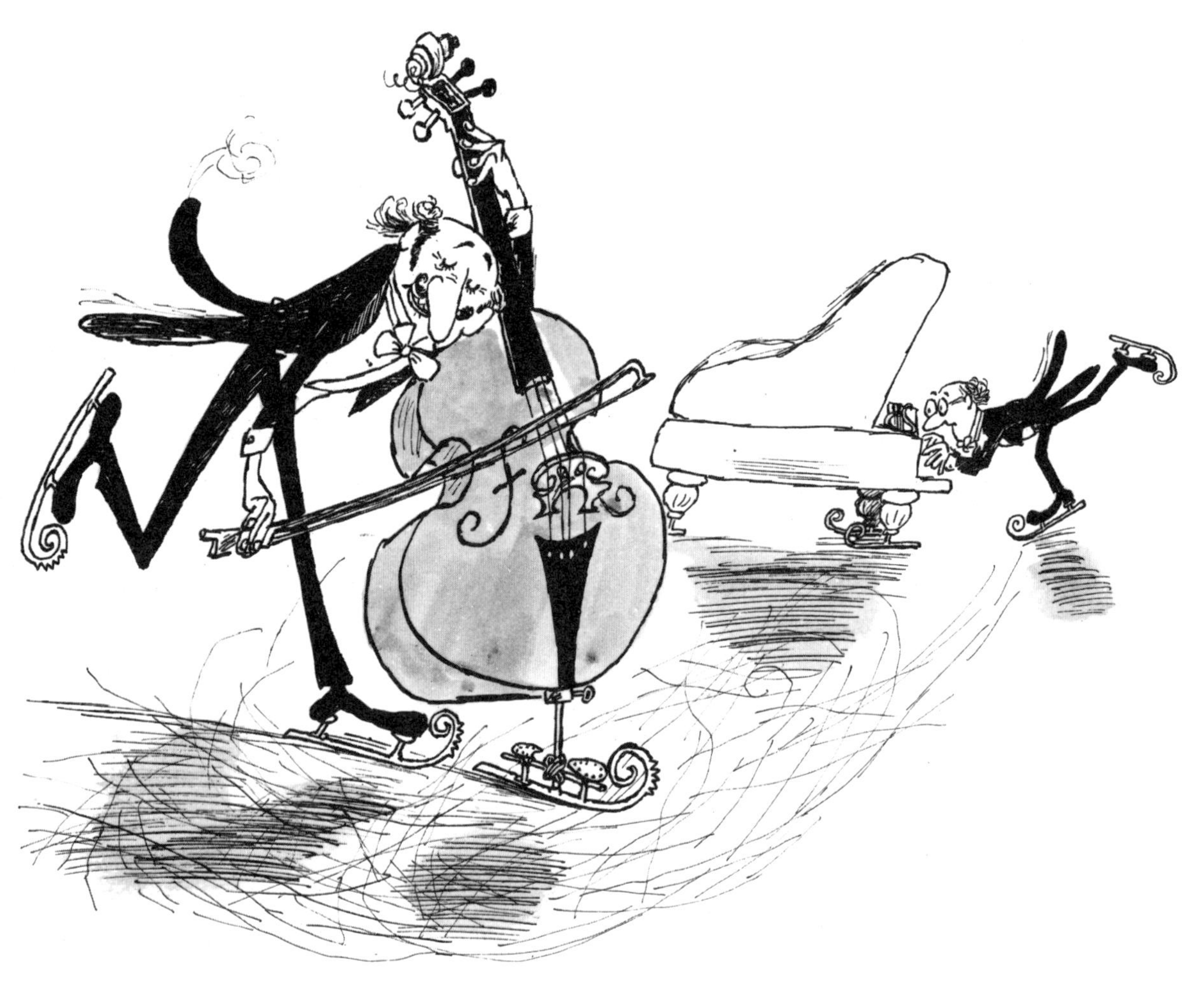

Skater's Waltz

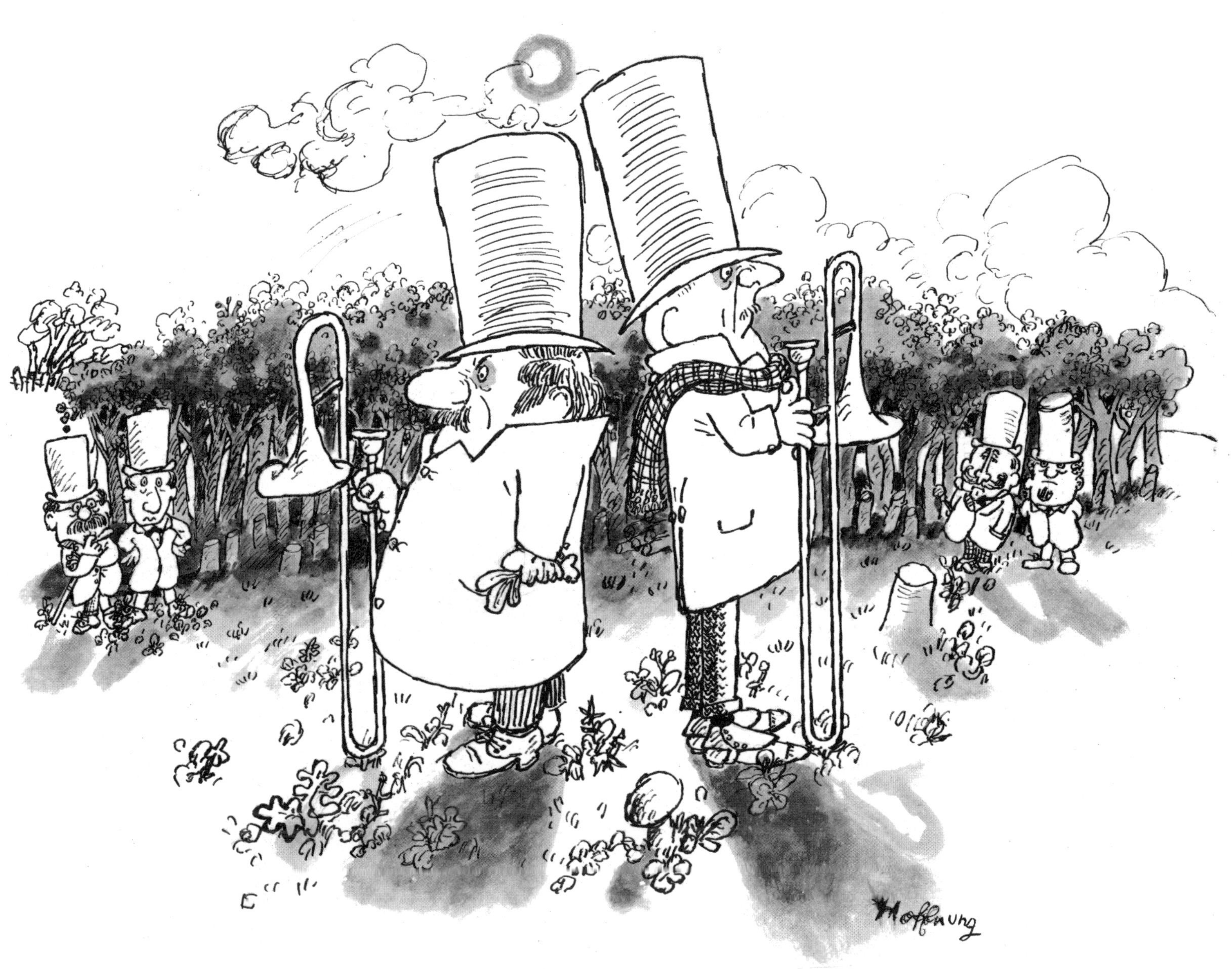
Hoffnung

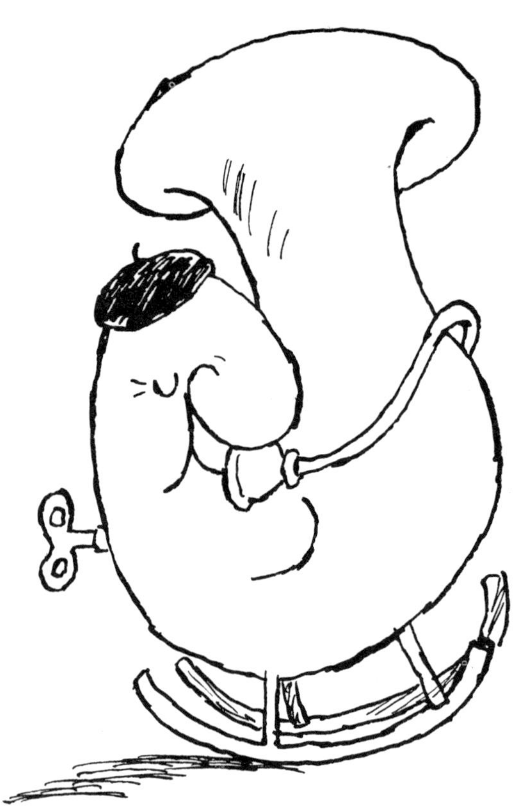

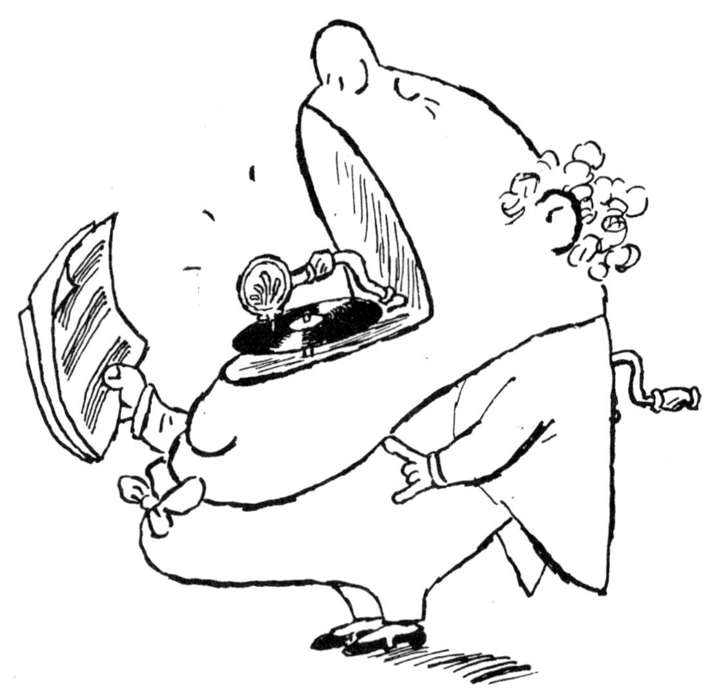

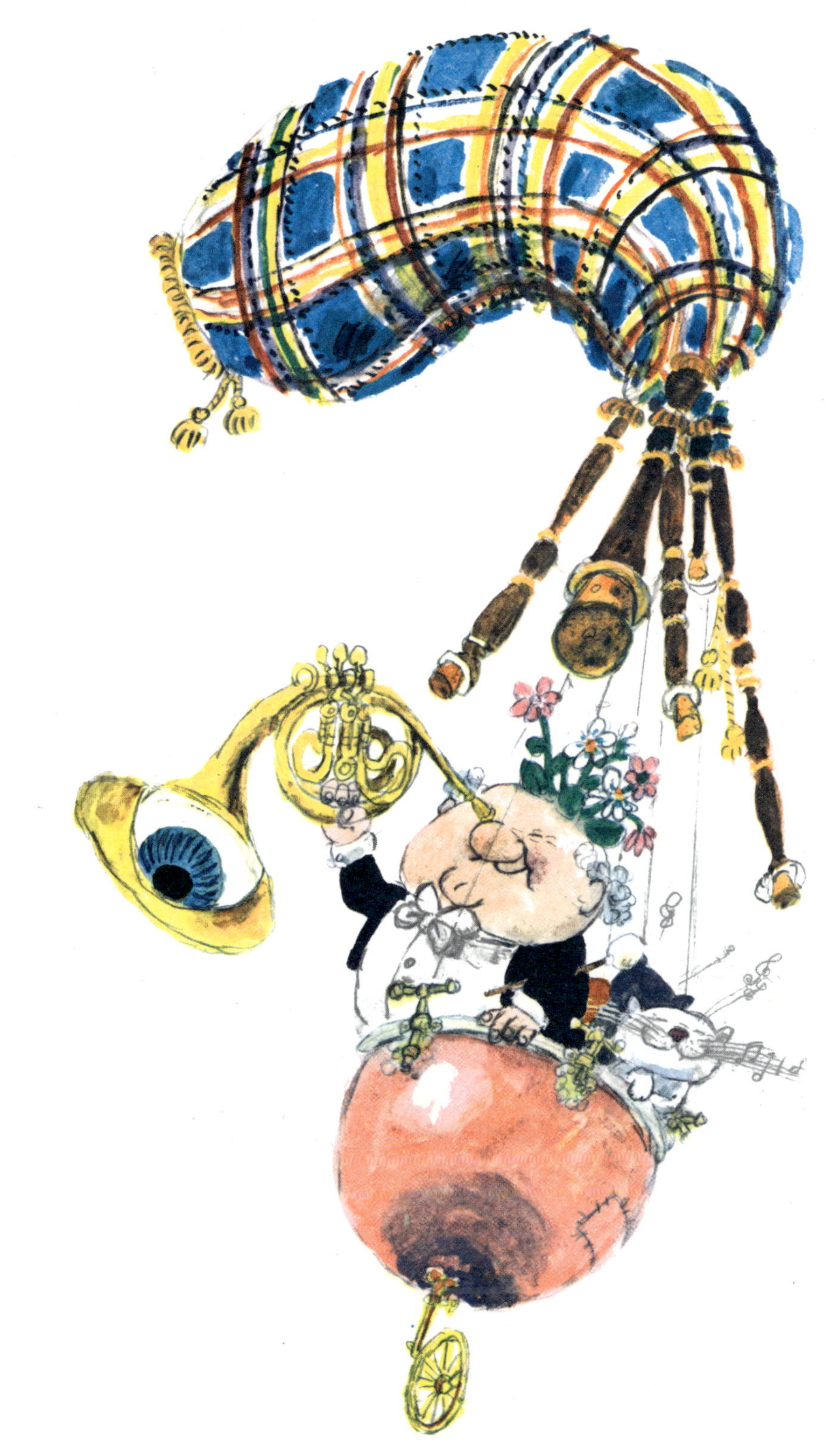

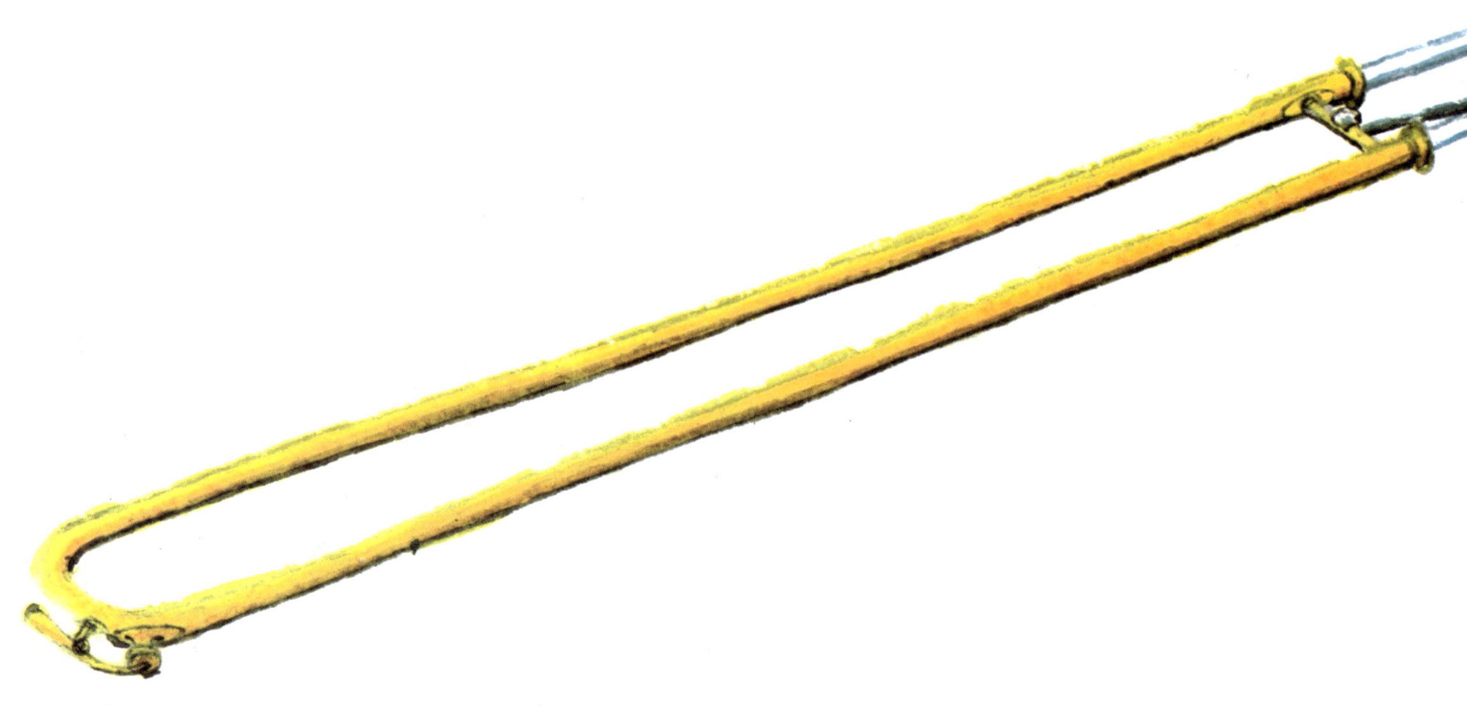

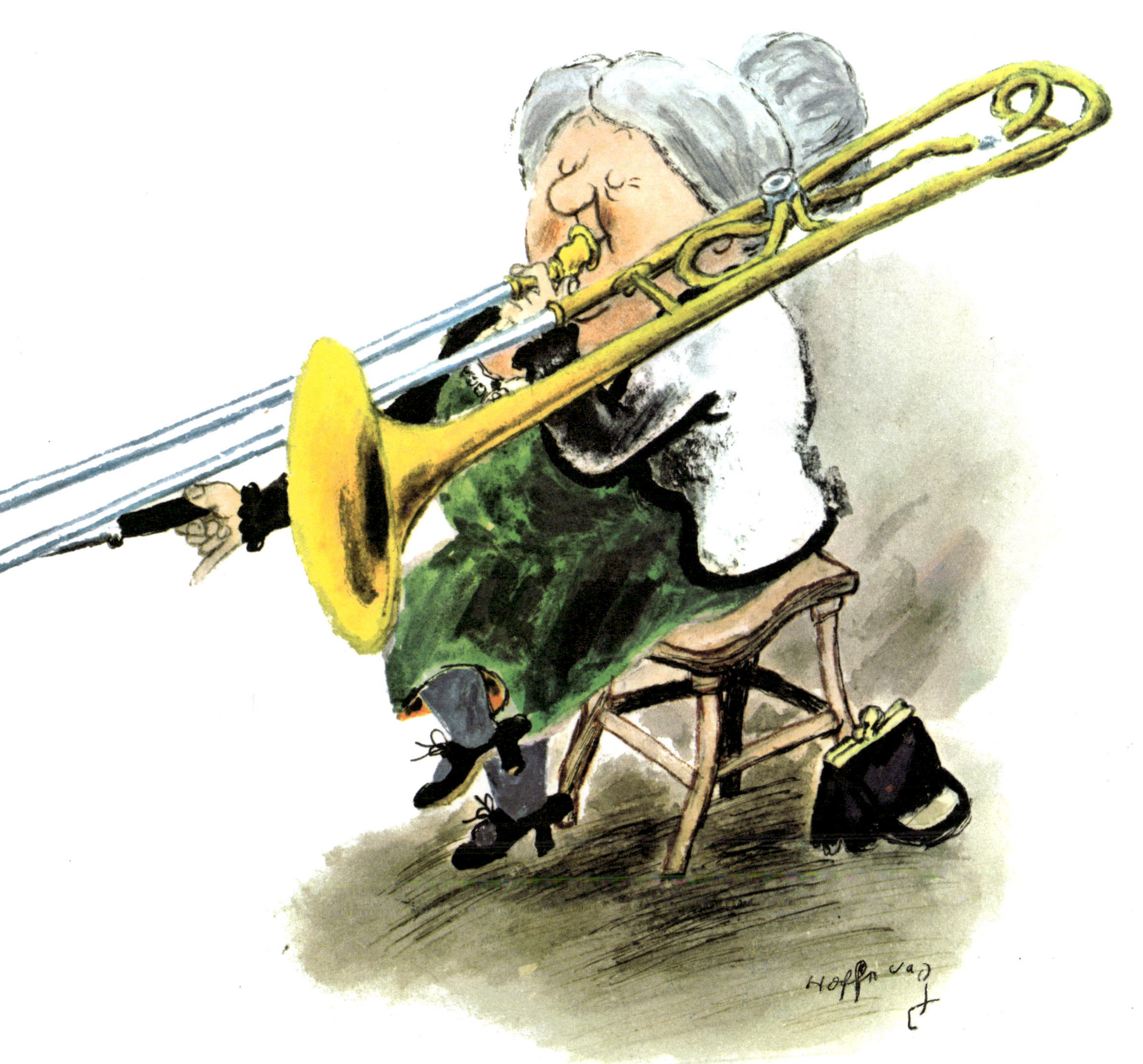

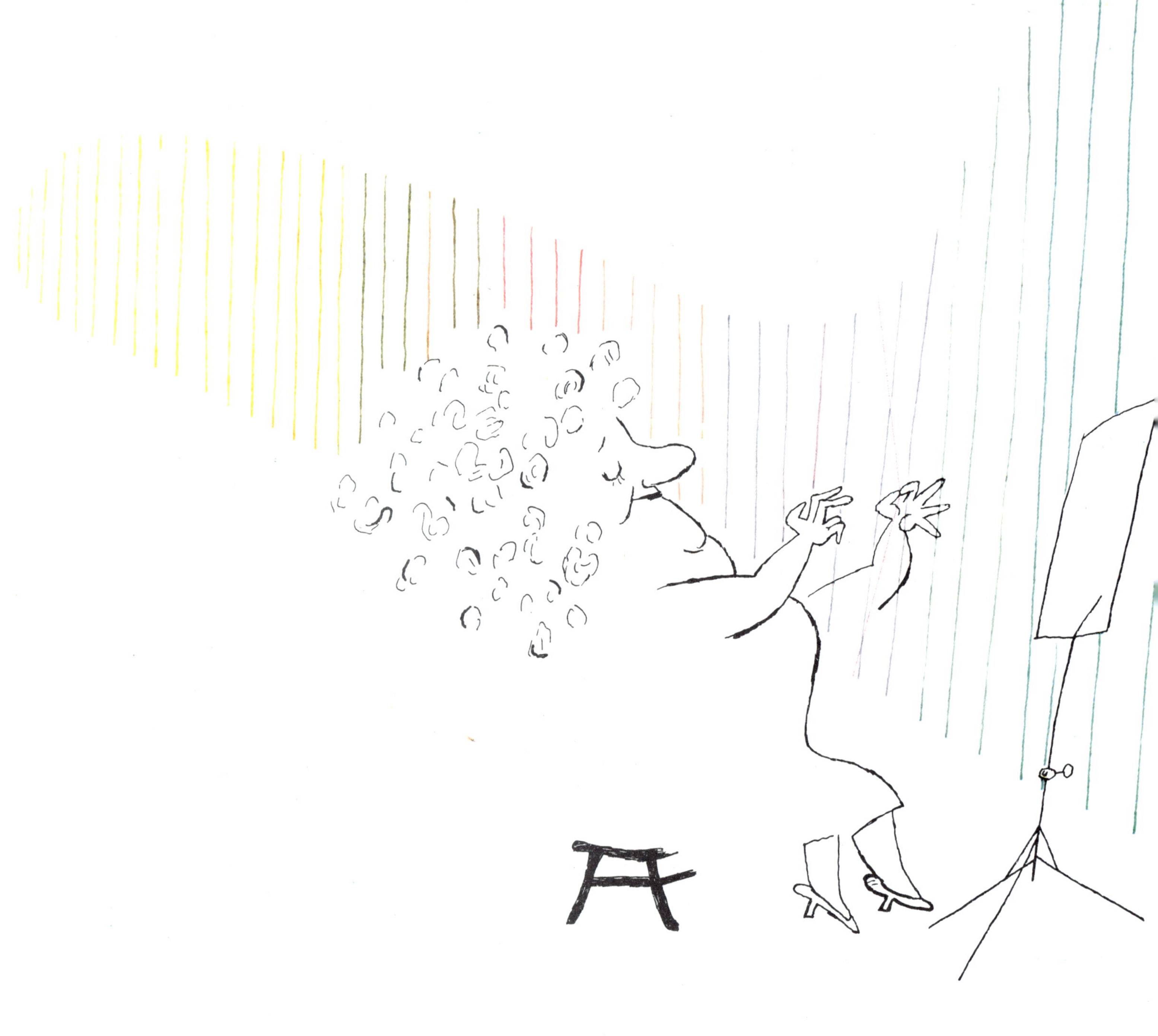

Hoffnung

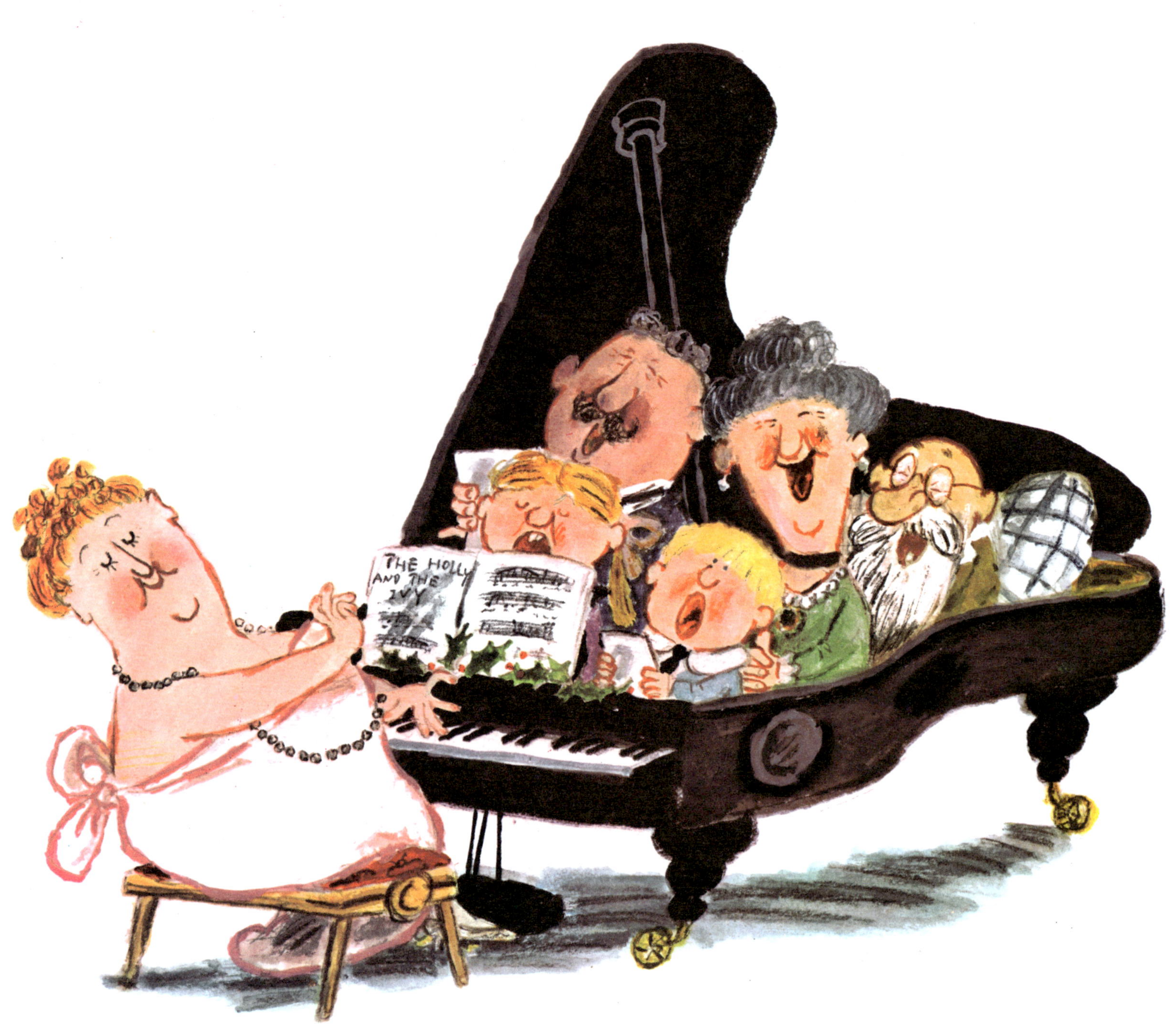
THE HOLLY AND THE IVY

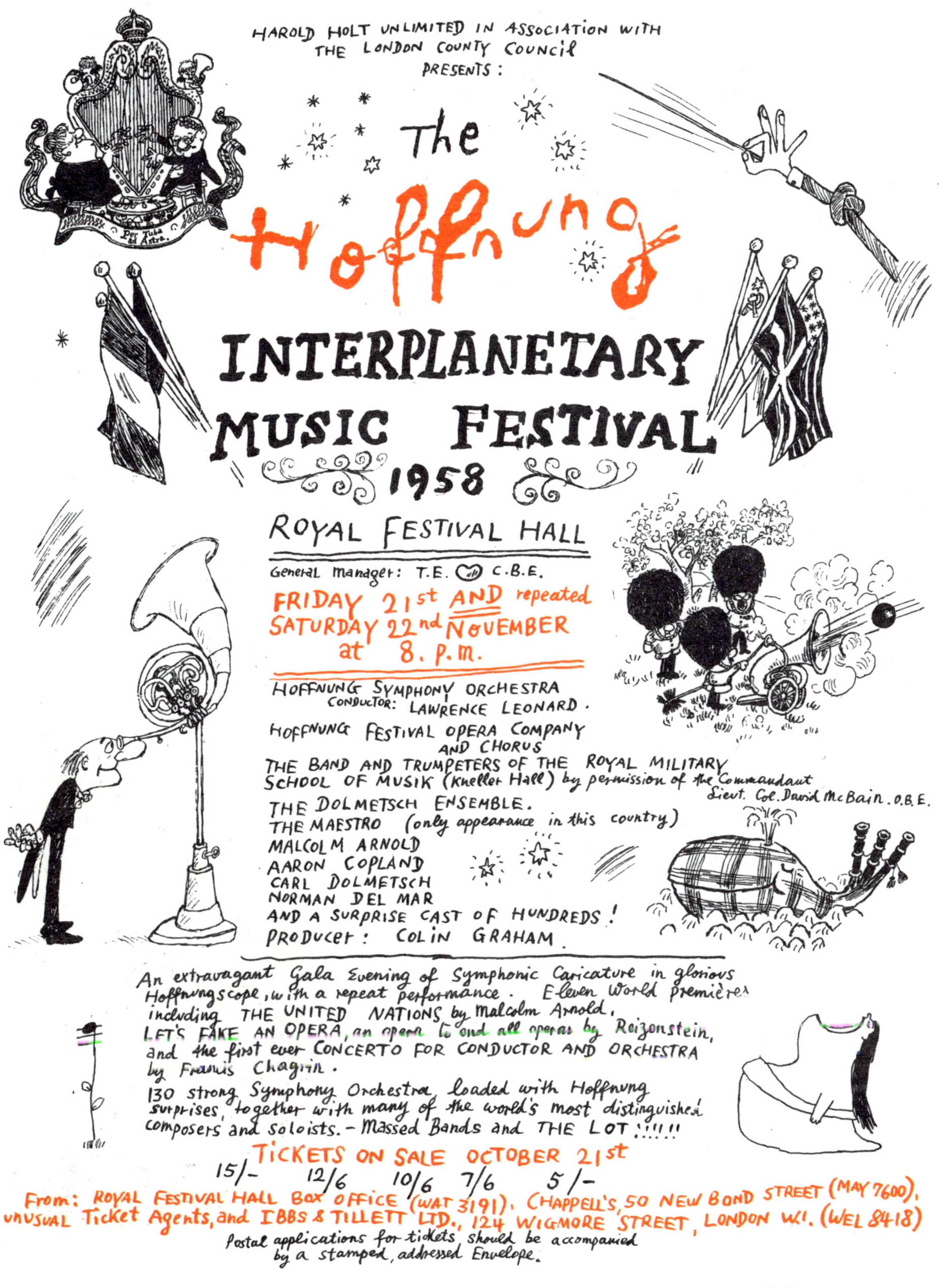

HAROLD HOLT UNLIMITED IN ASSOCIATION WITH
THE LONDON COUNTY COUNCIL
PRESENTS:
Per Tuba ad Astra.
The
Hoffnung
INTERPLANETARY
MUSIC FESTIVAL
1958
ROYAL FESTIVAL HALL
General Manager: T.E. C.B.E.
FRIDAY 21st AND repeated
SATURDAY 22nd NOVEMBER
at 8. p.m.
HOFFNUNG SYMPHONY ORCHESTRA
CONDUCTOR: LAWRENCE LEONARD.
HOFFNUNG FESTIVAL OPERA COMPANY
AND CHORUS
THE BAND AND TRUMPETERS OF THE ROYAL MILITARY
SCHOOL OF MUSIK (Kneller Hall) by permission of the Commandant
Lieut. Col. David McBain. O.B.E.
THE DOLMETSCH ENSEMBLE.
THE MAESTRO (only appearance in this country)
MALCOLM ARNOLD
AARON COPLAND
CARL DOLMETSCH
NORMAN DEL MAR
AND A SURPRISE CAST OF HUNDREDS!
PRODUCER: COLIN GRAHAM.
An extravagant Gala Evening of Symphonic Caricature in glorious
Hoffnungscope, with a repeat performance. Eleven World premières
including THE UNITED NATIONS by Malcolm Arnold,
LET'S FAKE AN OPERA, an opera to end all operas by Reizenstein,
and the first ever CONCERTO FOR CONDUCTOR AND ORCHESTRA
by Francis Chagrin.
130 strong Symphony Orchestra, loaded with Hoffnung
surprises, together with many of the world's most distinguished
composers and soloists. - Massed Bands and THE LOT!!!!!!
TICKETS ON SALE OCTOBER 21st
15/- 12/6 10/6 7/6 5/-
From: ROYAL FESTIVAL HALL BOX OFFICE (WAT 3191). CHAPPELL'S, 50 NEW BOND STREET (MAY 7600),
USUAL Ticket Agents, and IBBS & TILLETT LTD., 124 WIGMORE STREET, LONDON W.1. (WEL 8418)
Postal applications for tickets should be accompanied
by a stamped, addressed Envelope.
DRAWINGS REPRODUCED FROM
THE HOFFNUNG CARTOON BOOKS,
BY PERMISSION OF DOBSON - PUTNAM.

The Dragon, for:
"Let's fake an Opera"

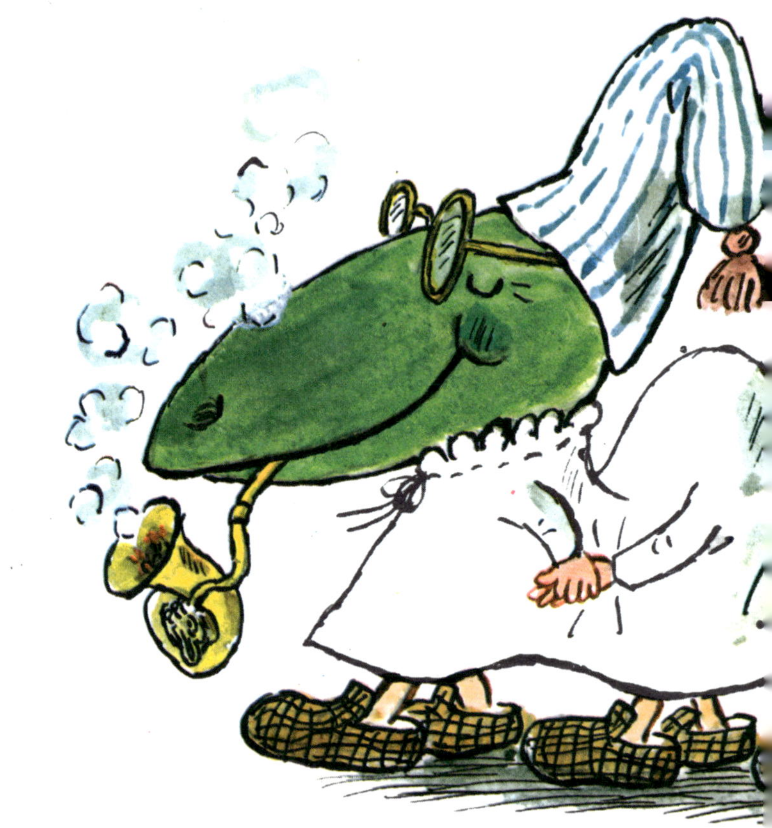

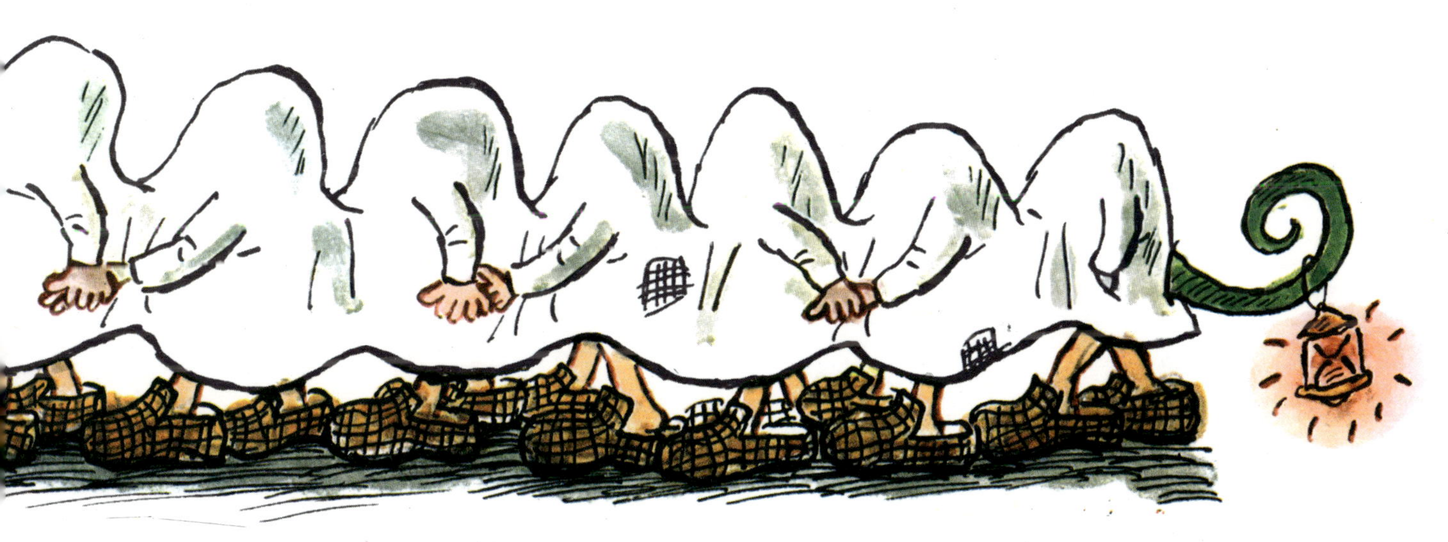

Glyndebourne

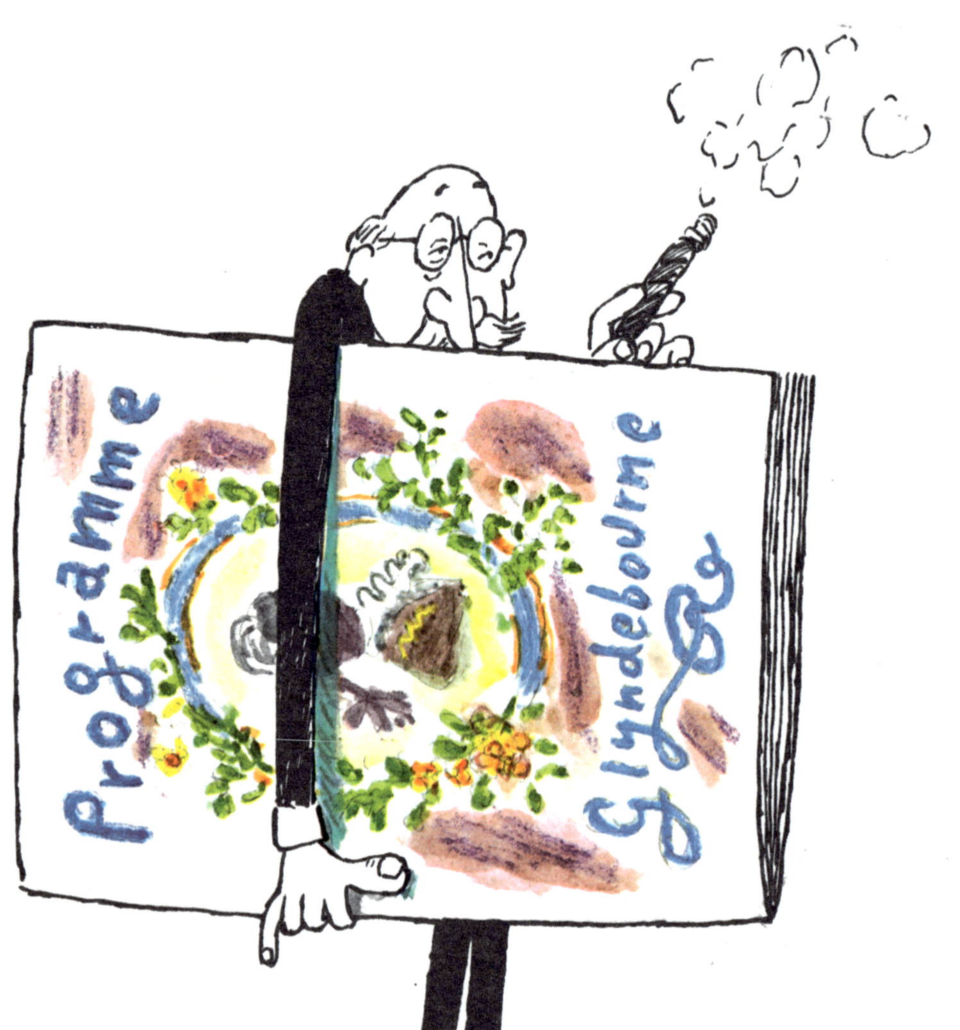

Lavishly illustrated programmes are on sale everywhere.

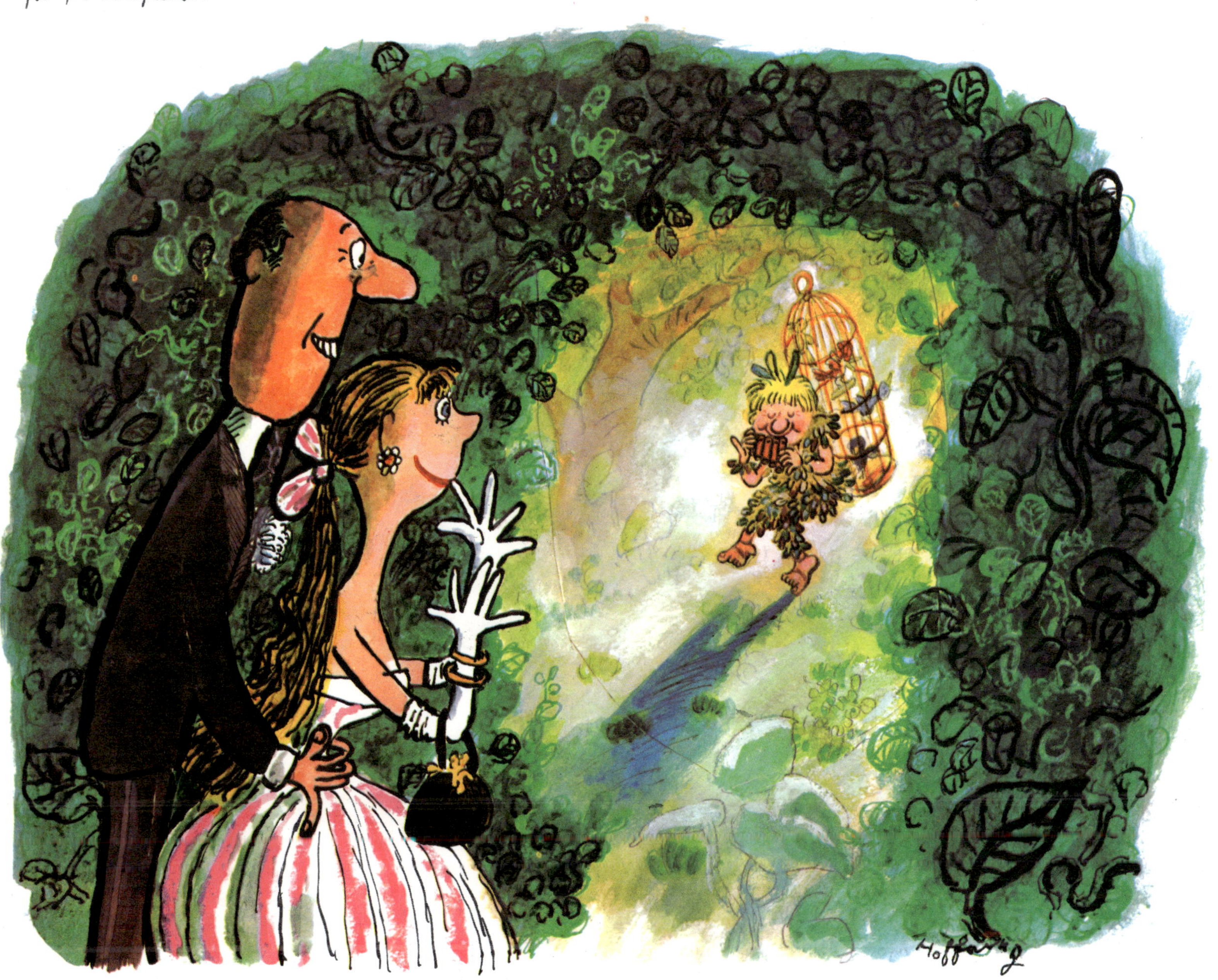

7. Wandering about the Grounds, the visitor must be prepared for the unexpected.

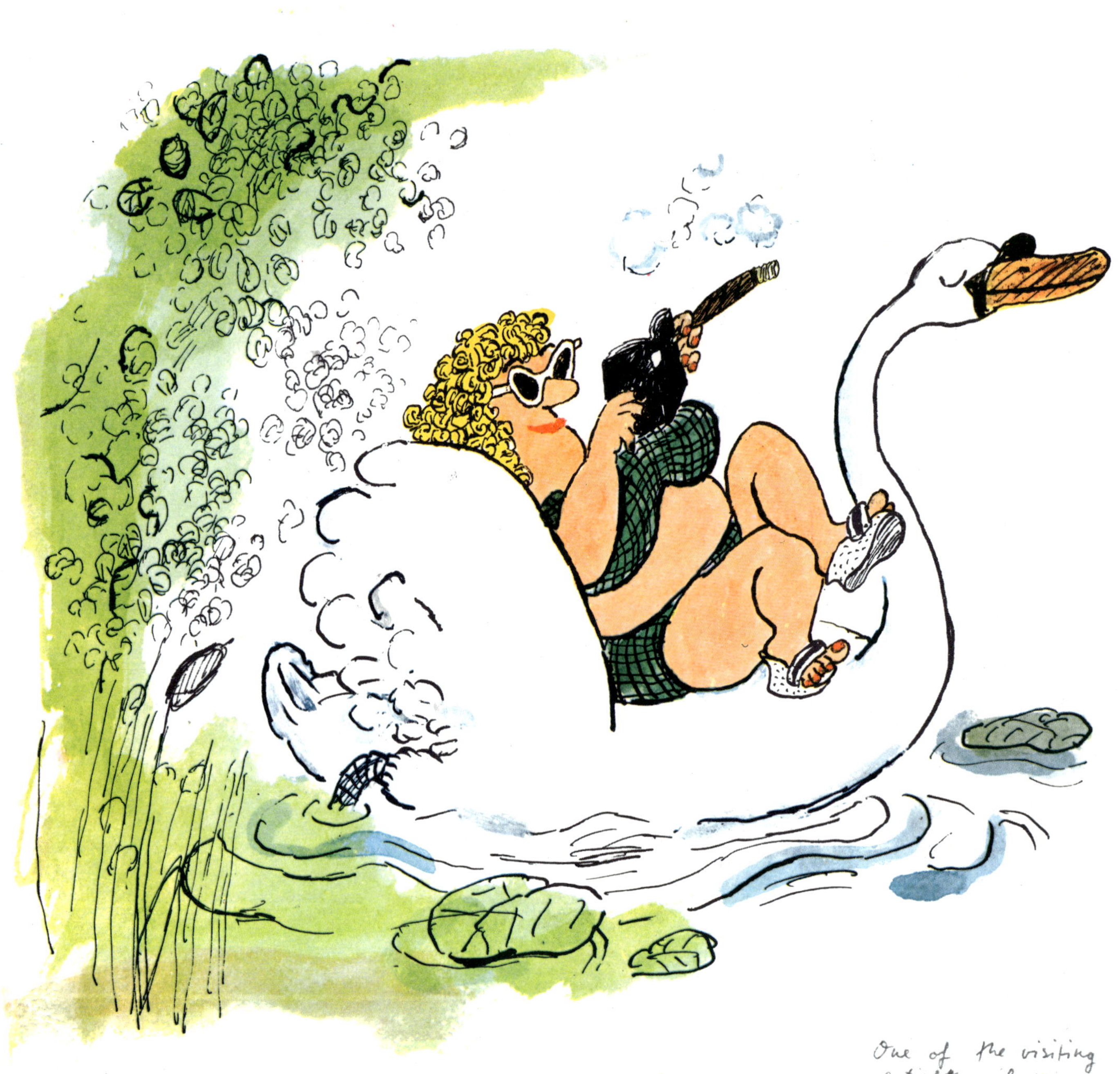

One of the visiting artists relaxes.

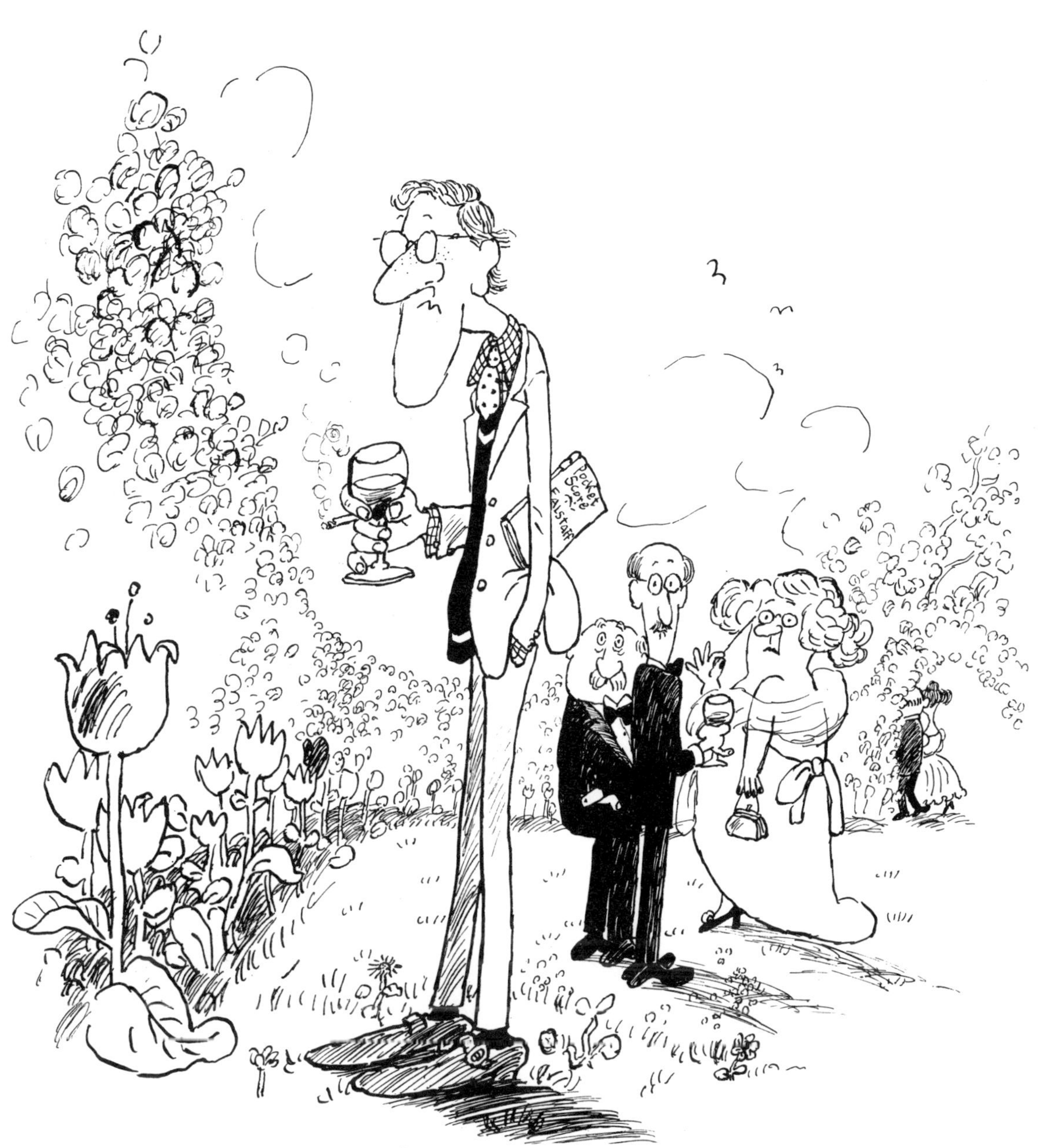

Evening dress is optional.

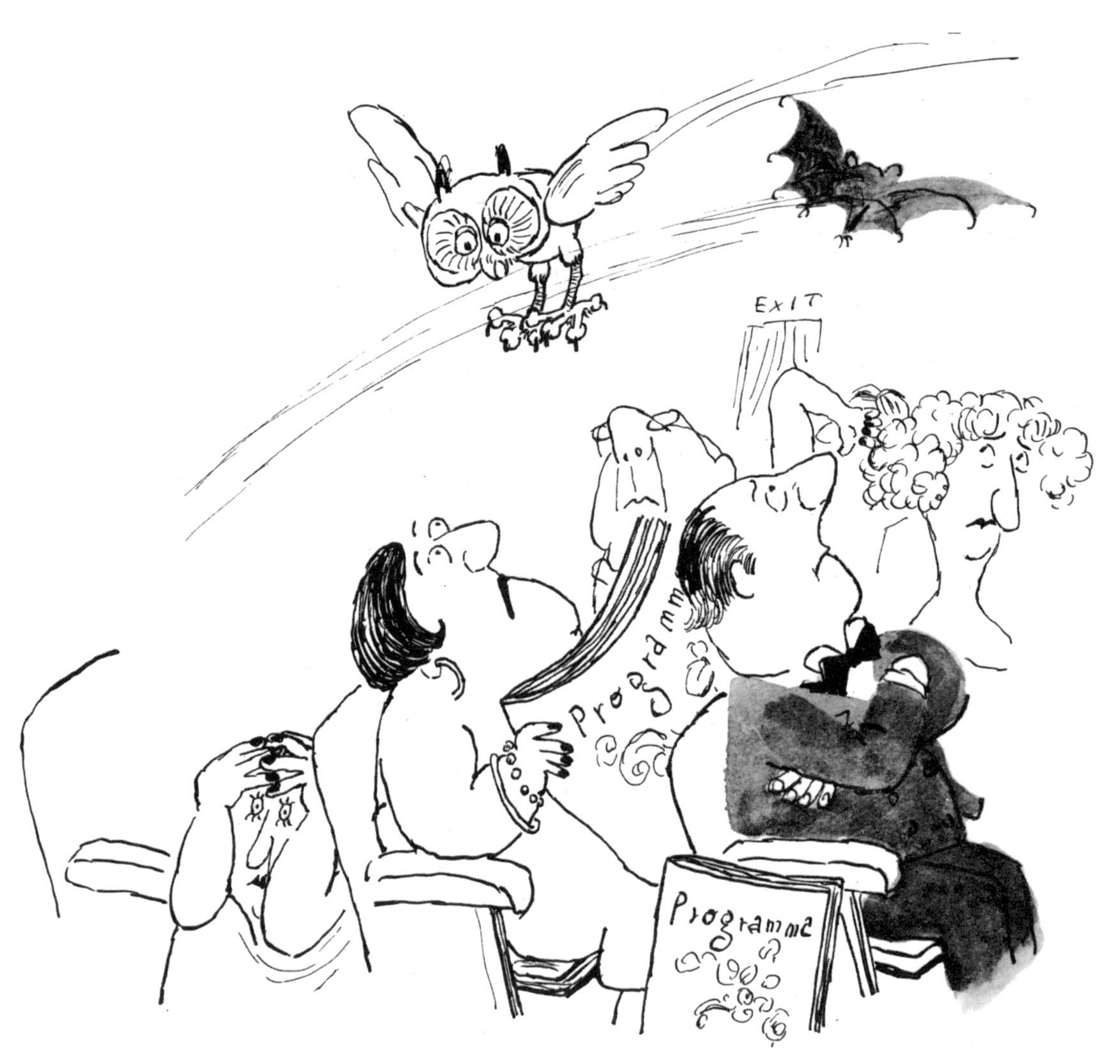

In Keeping with the rest of Glyndebourne, the auditorium has atmospherics of its own.

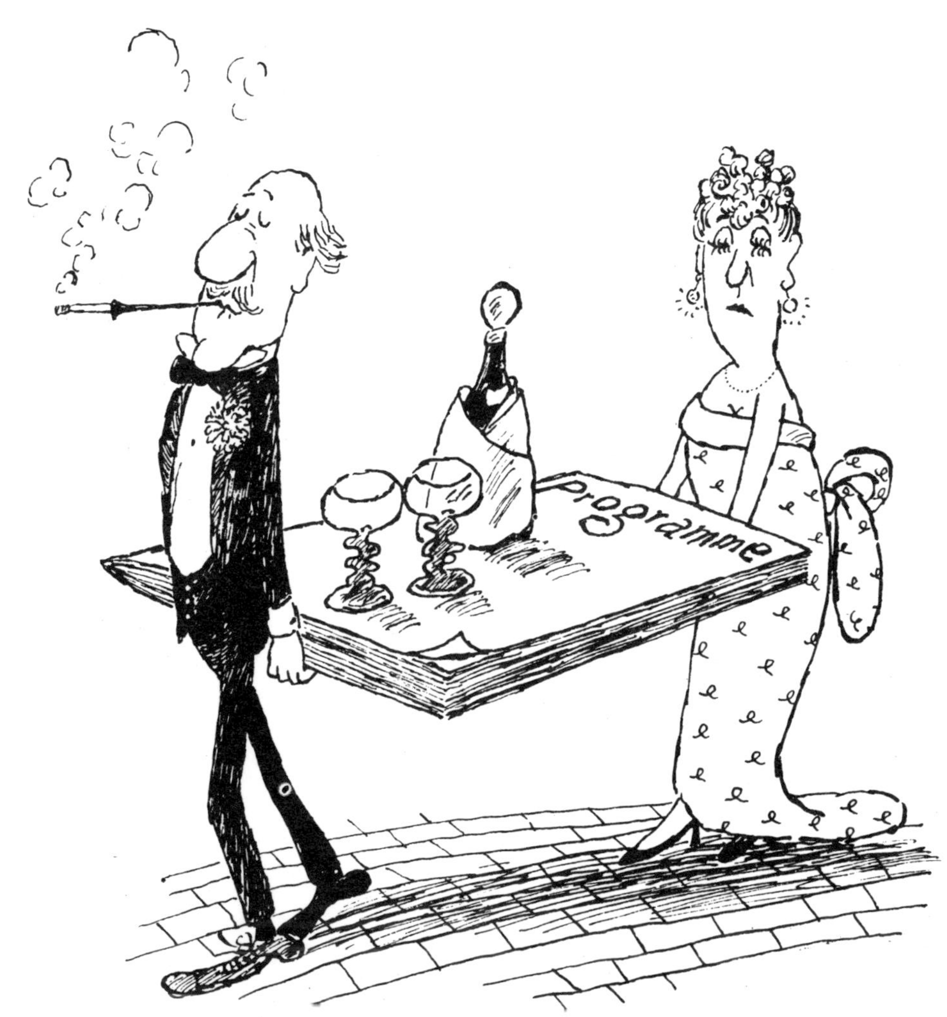
Programme

Artistes take full advantage of Sussex countryside

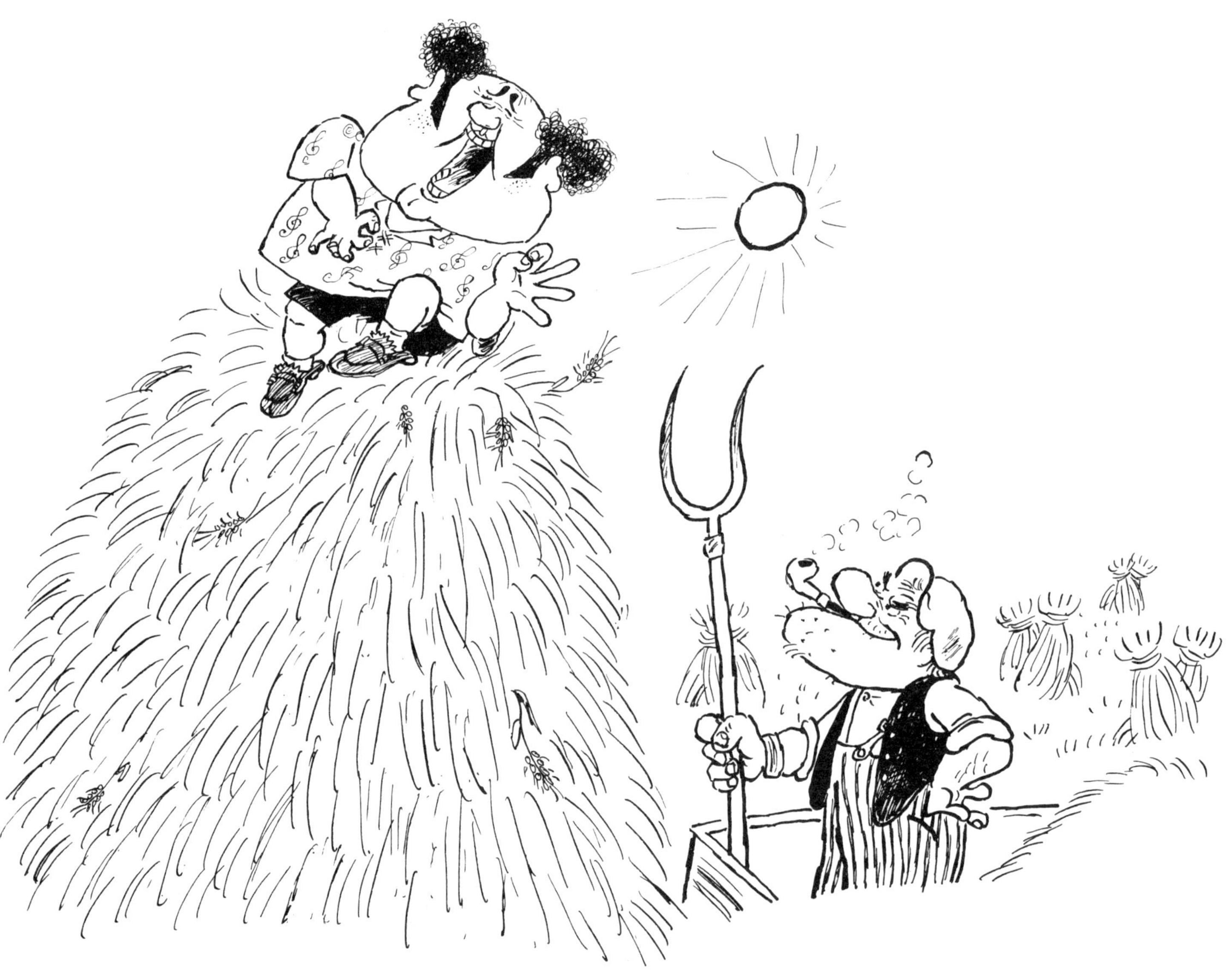

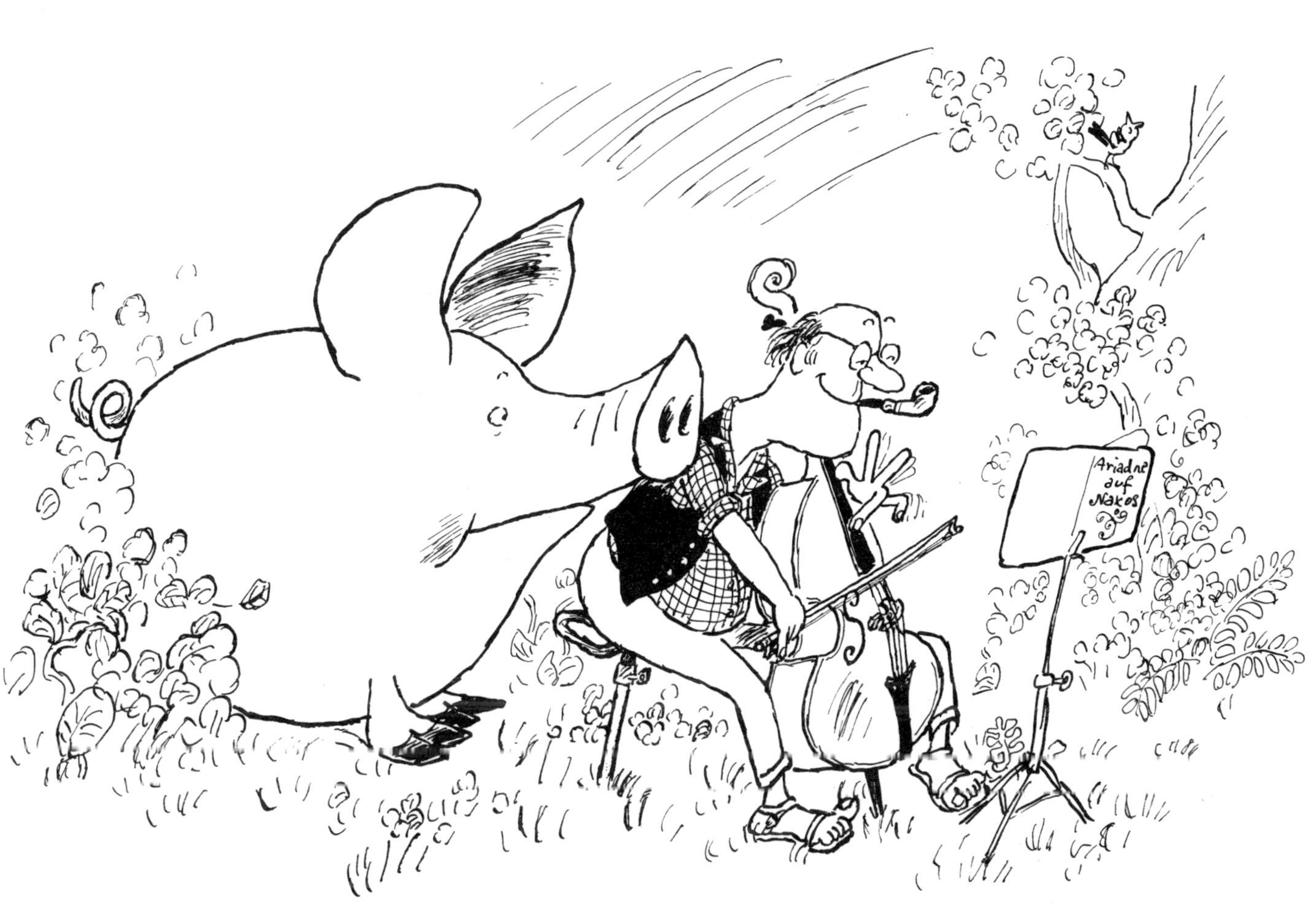
Ariadne
auf
Nakos

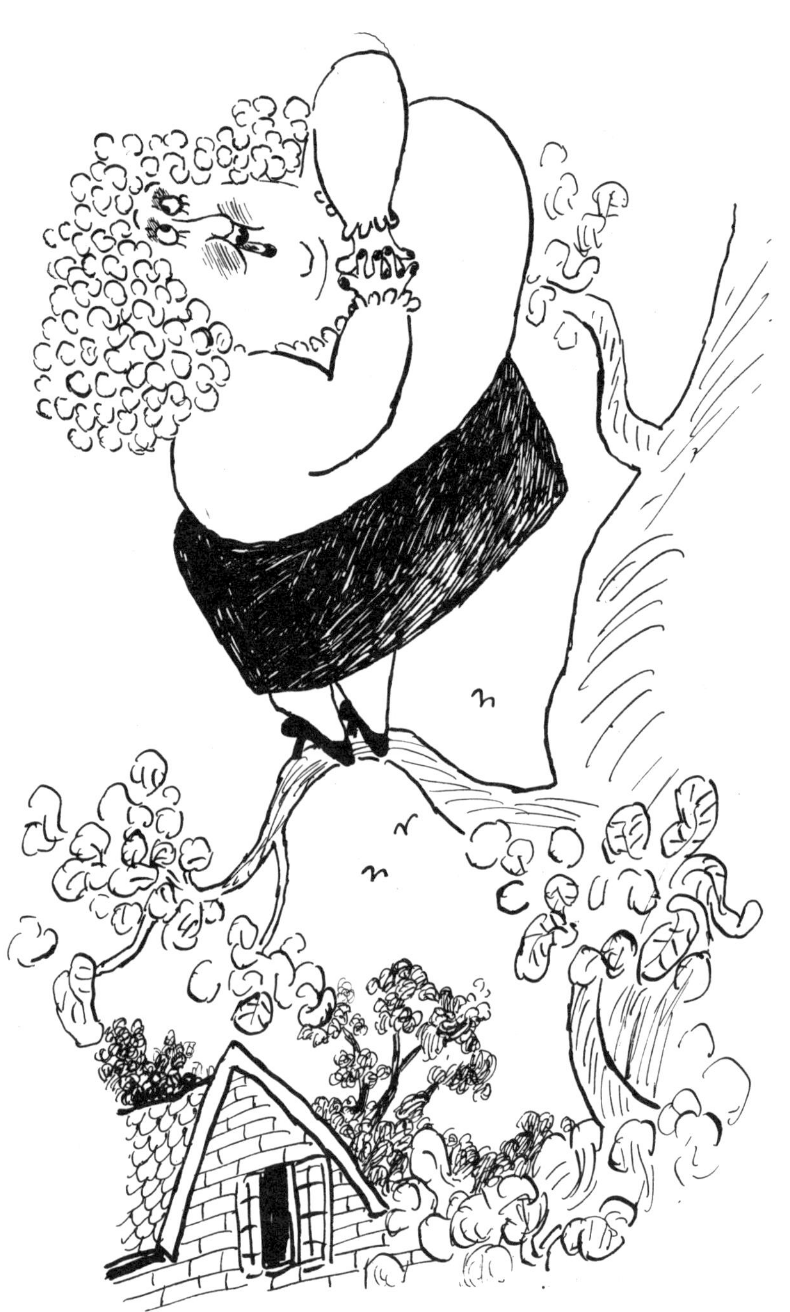

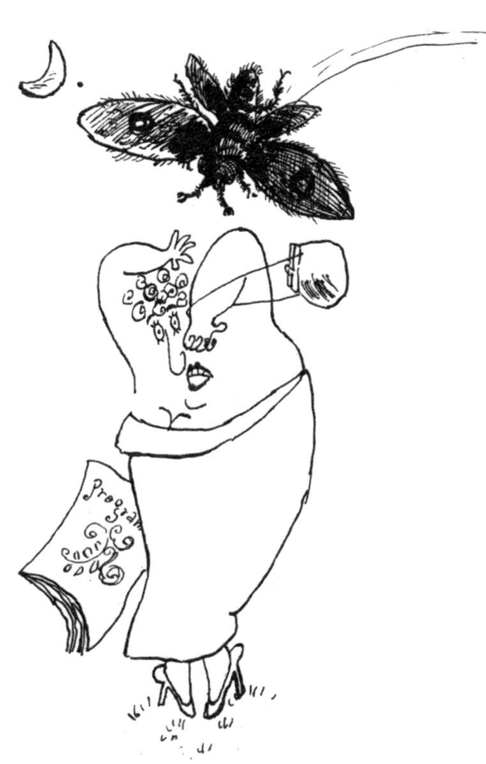

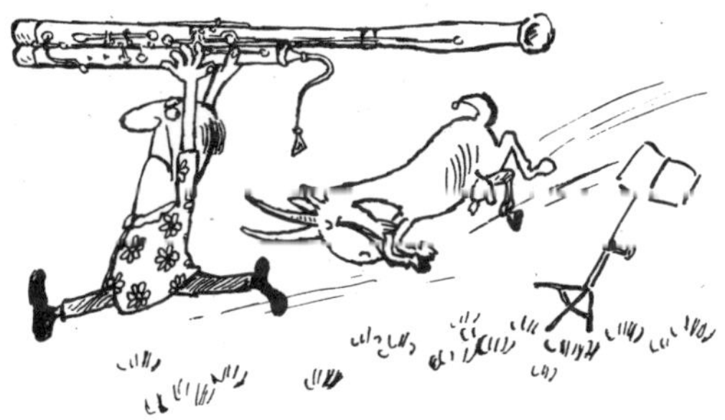

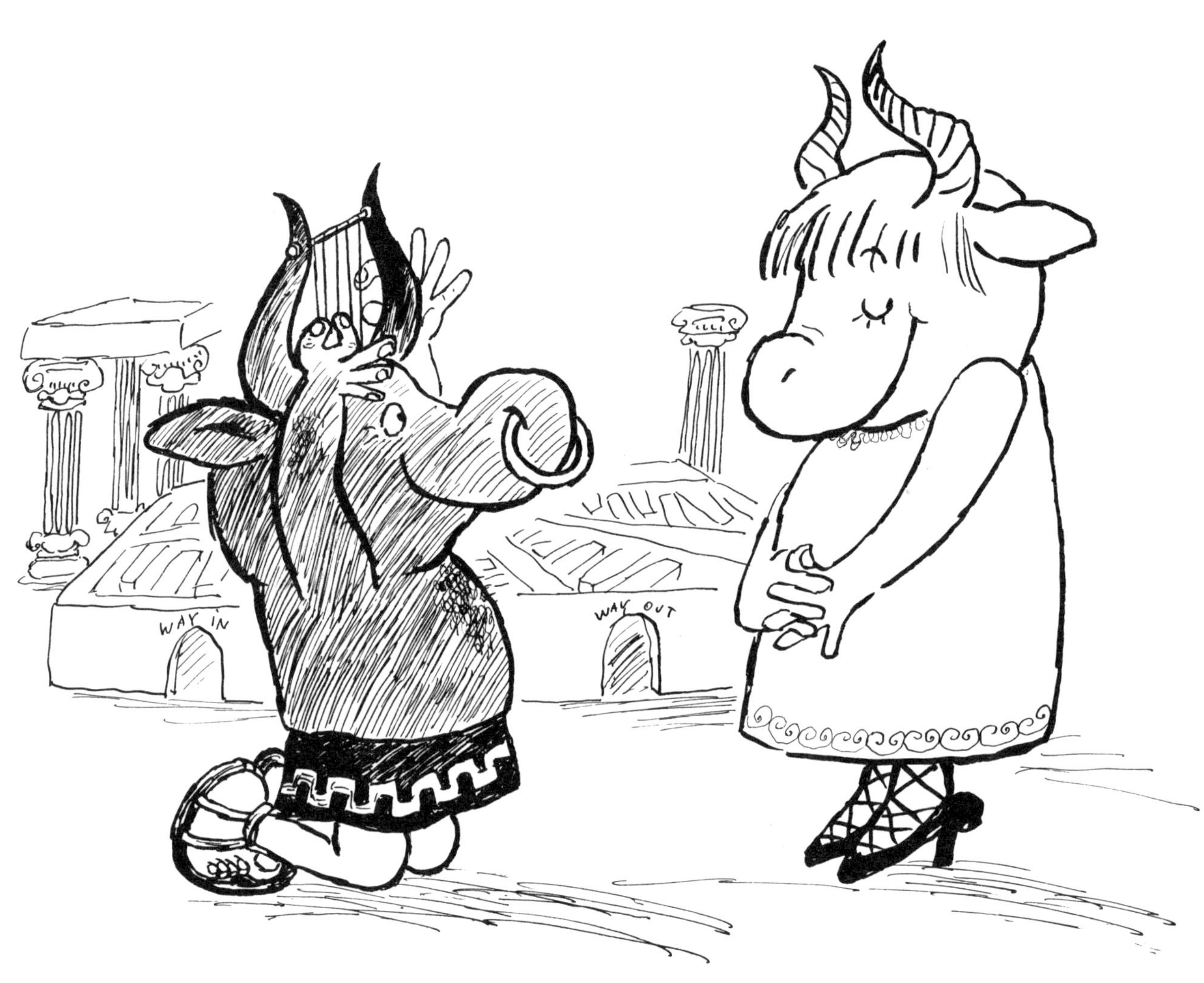
WAY IN
WAY OUT

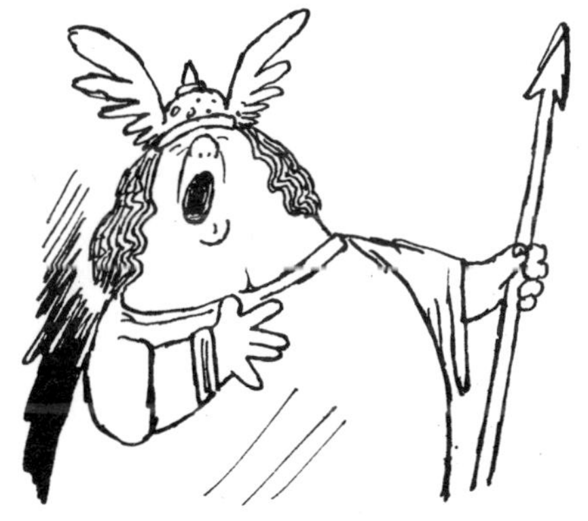

. . . how hotly
Caruso put on the motley.

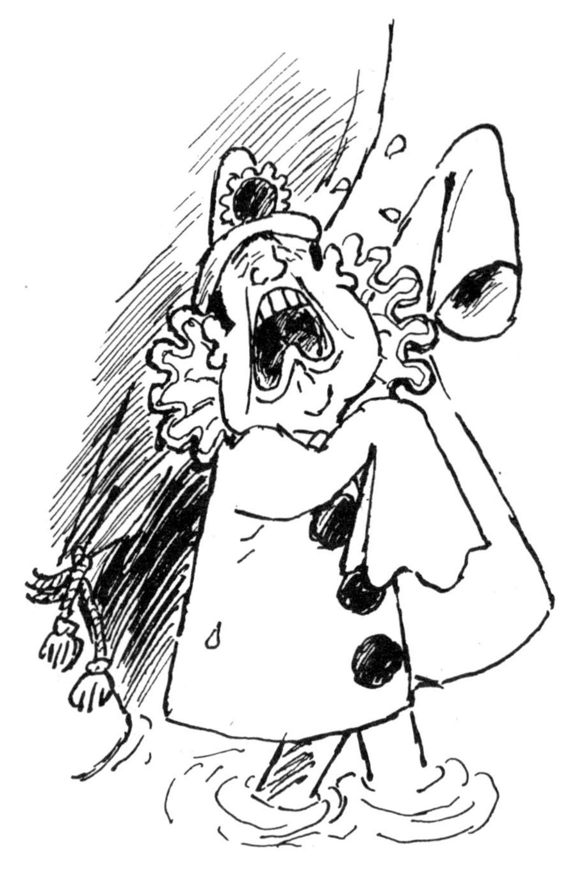

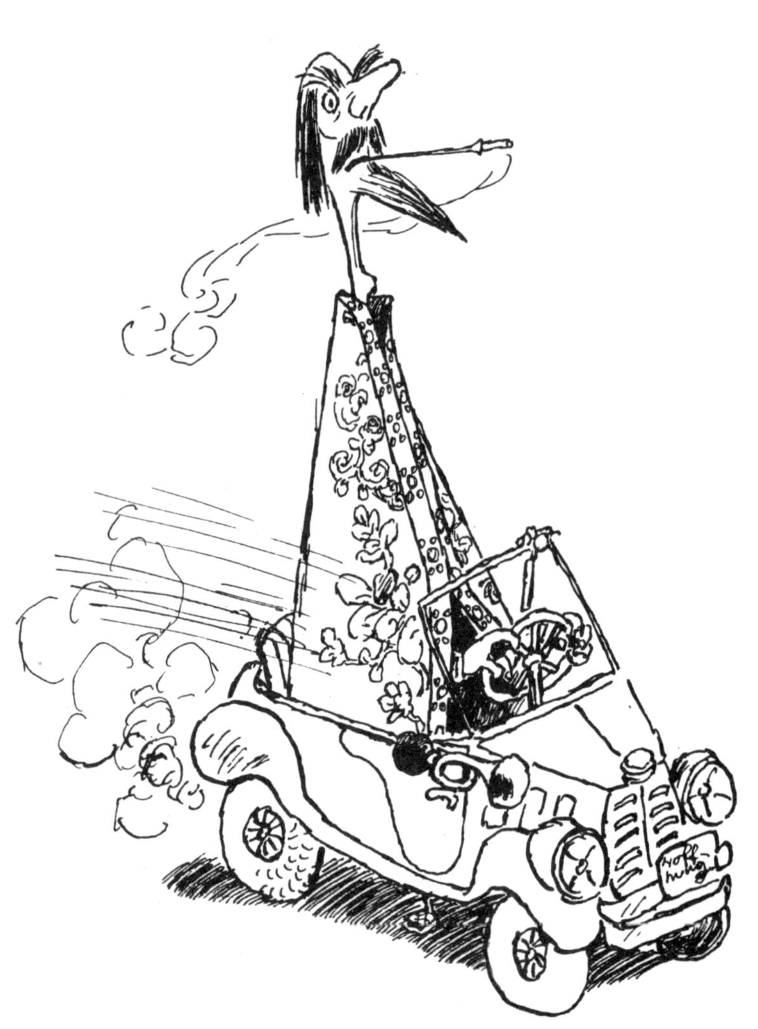

Boris Godounoff
Took the afternounoff.

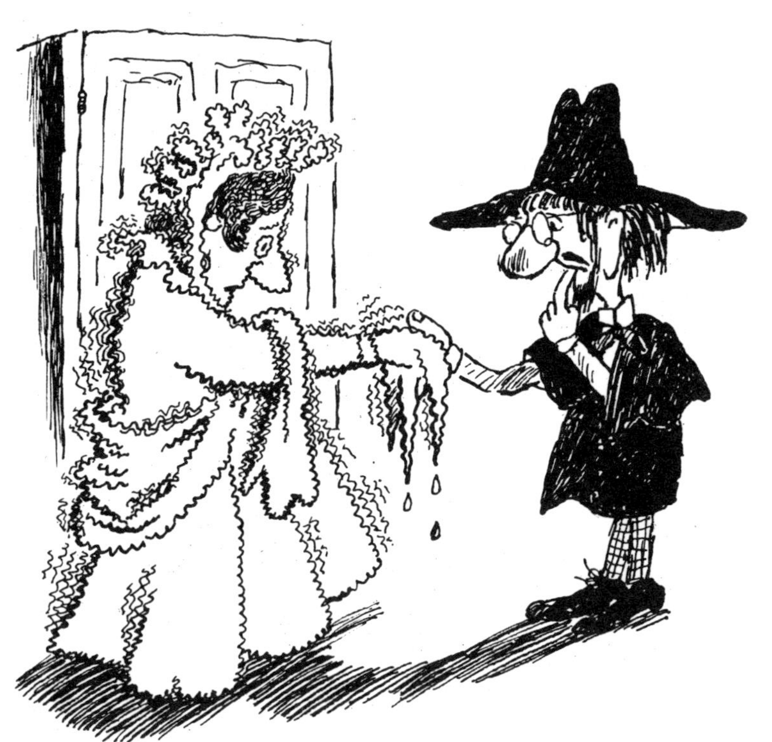

..... Rudolph had never seen a more GELIDA MANINA.

... Sparafucile ....

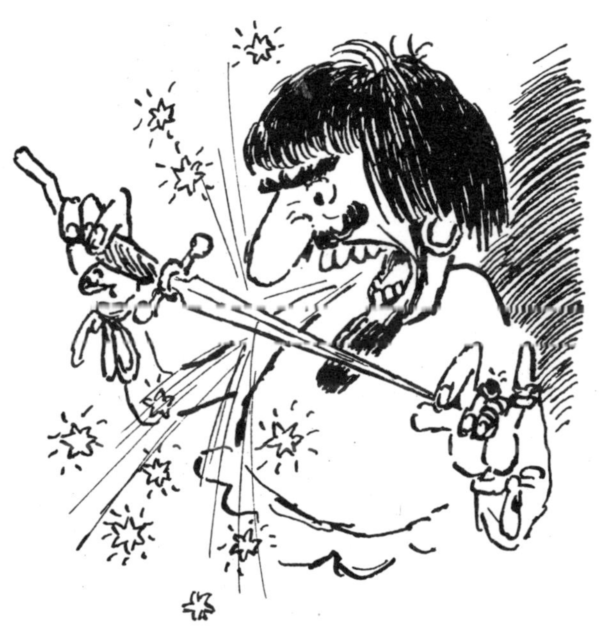

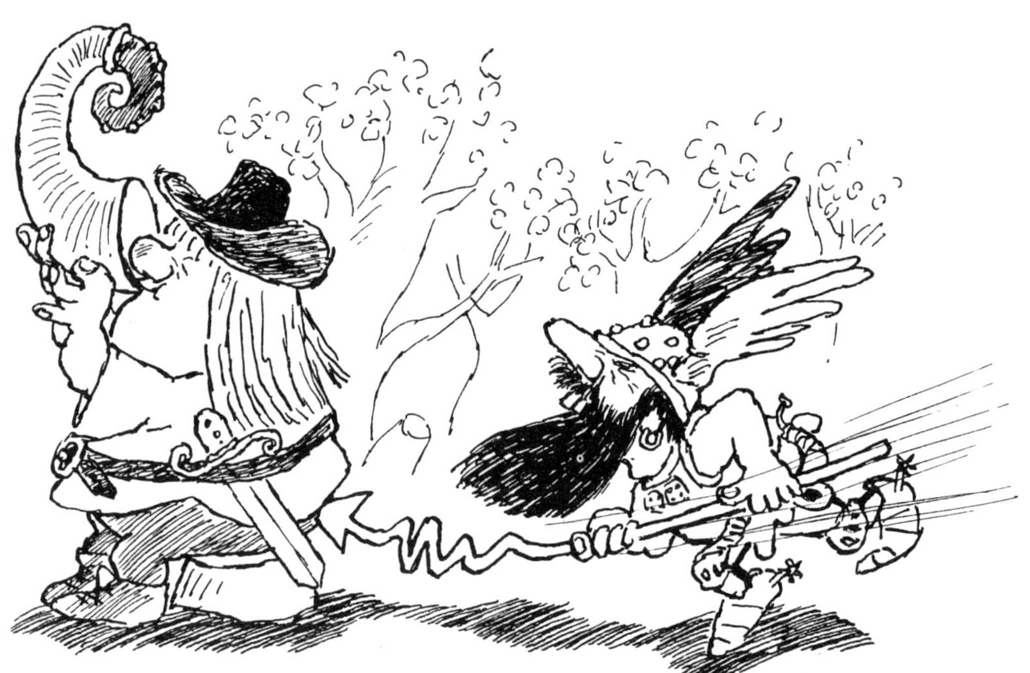

Hagen
drove a very
hard bargain.....

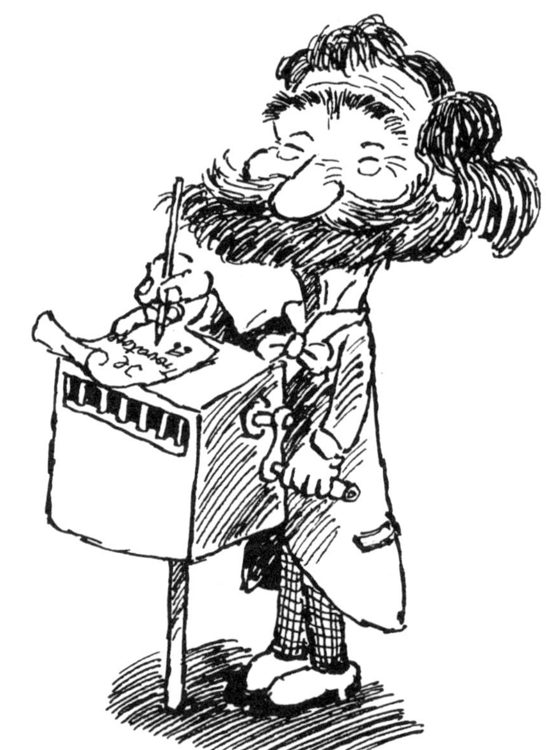

Guiseppe Verdi
Scored his early operas a la hurdy-gurdy

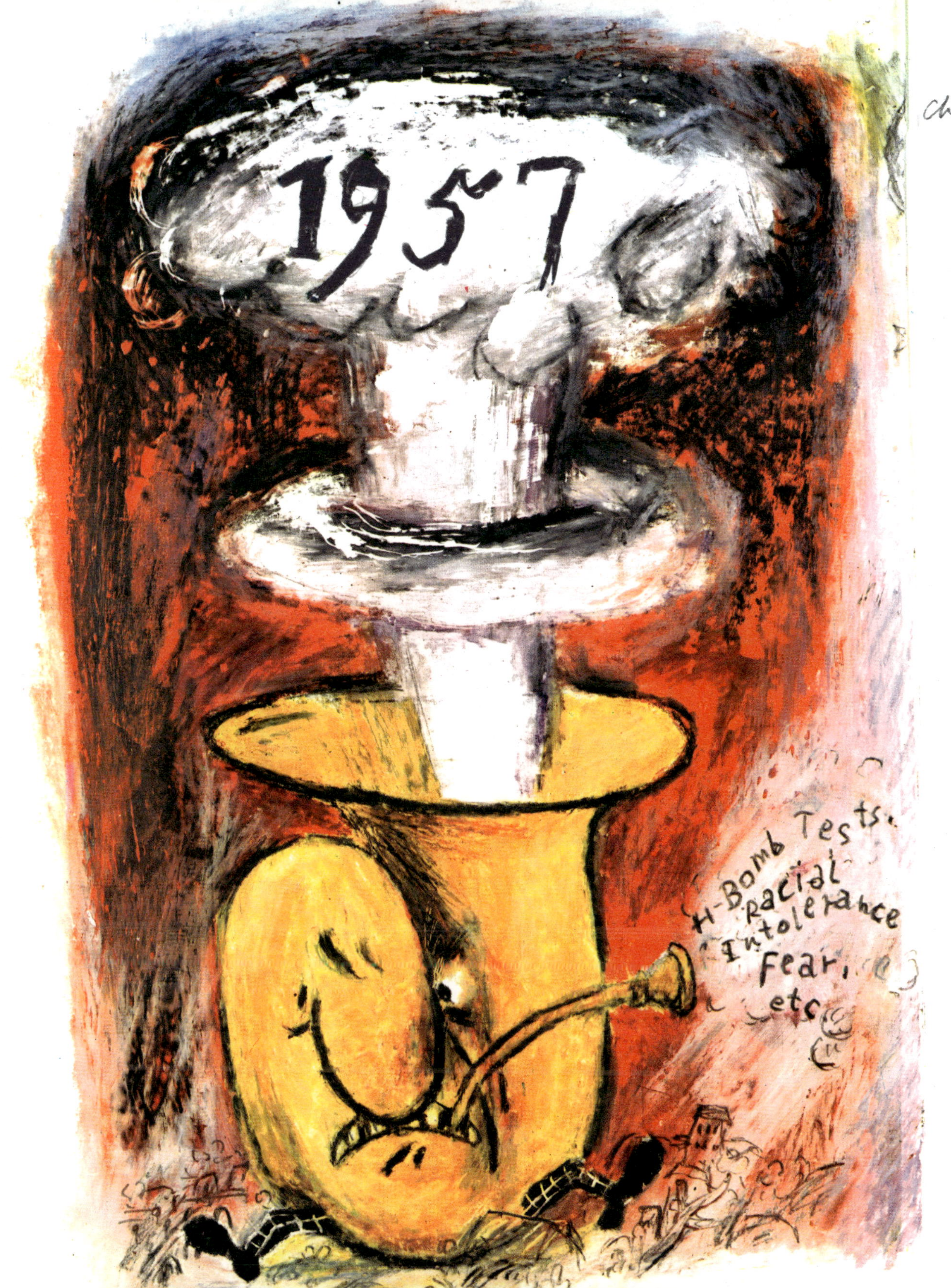

Chelsea Arts Ball

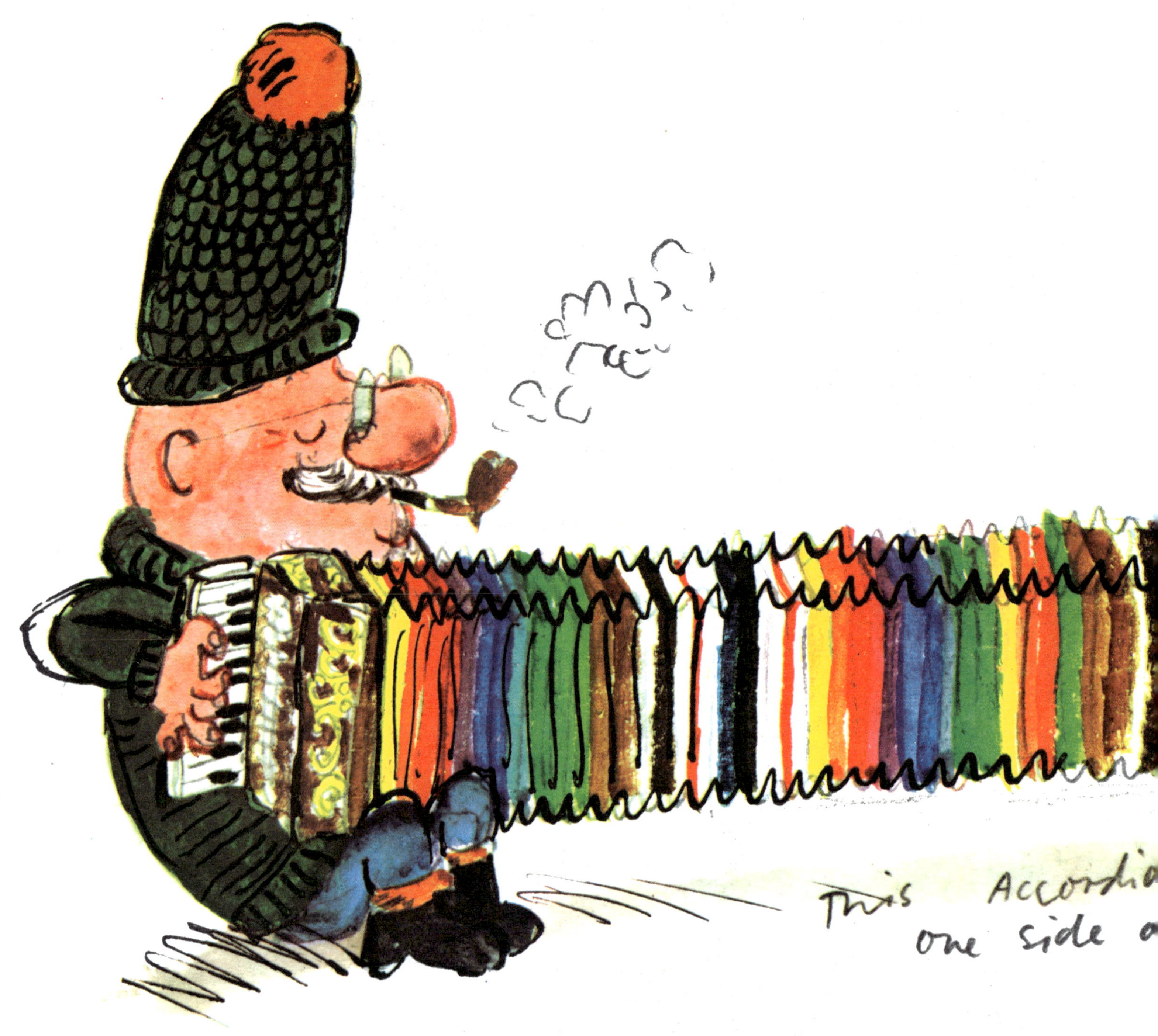
This Accordia
one side o

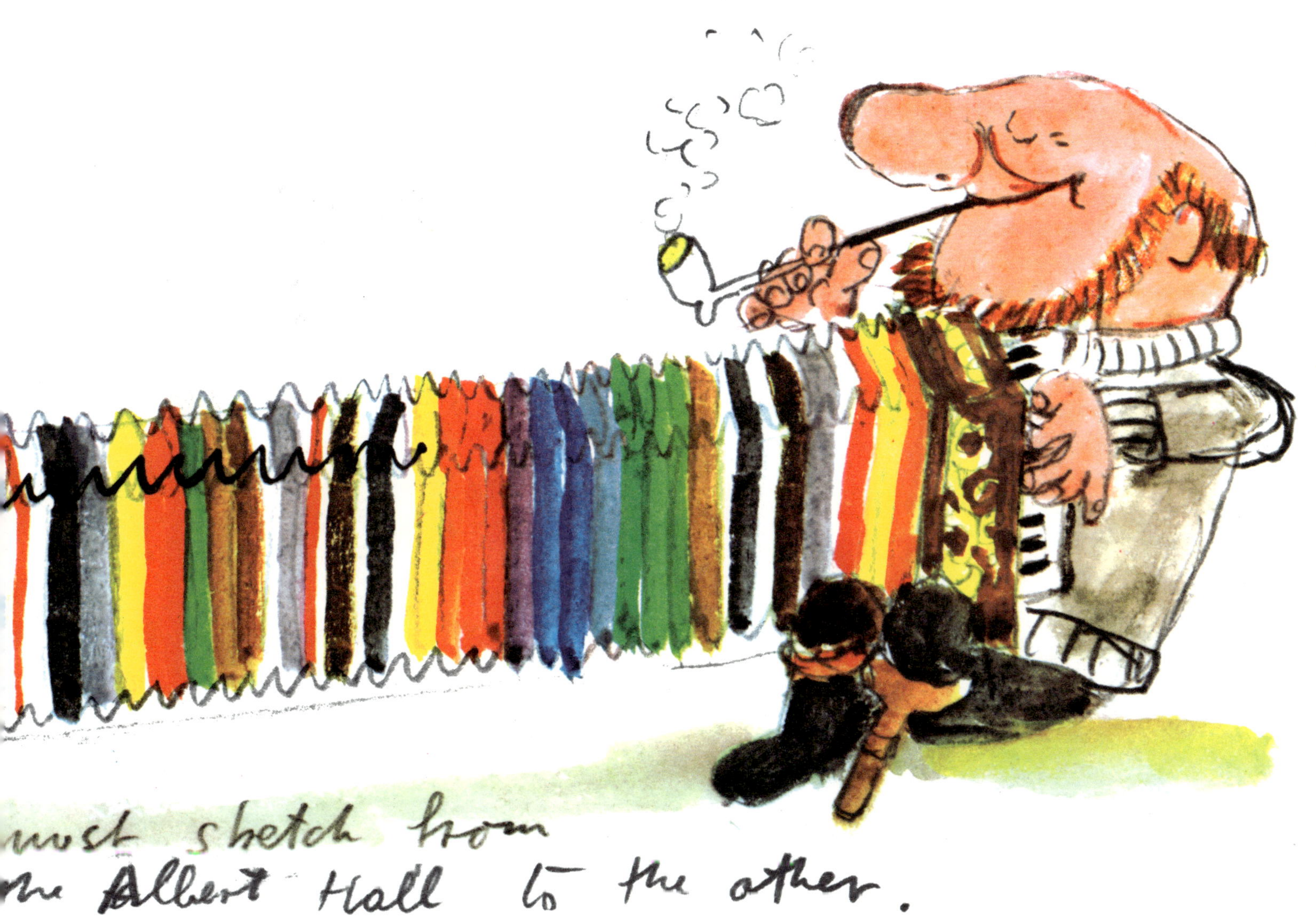

most sketch from
ne Albert Hall to the other.

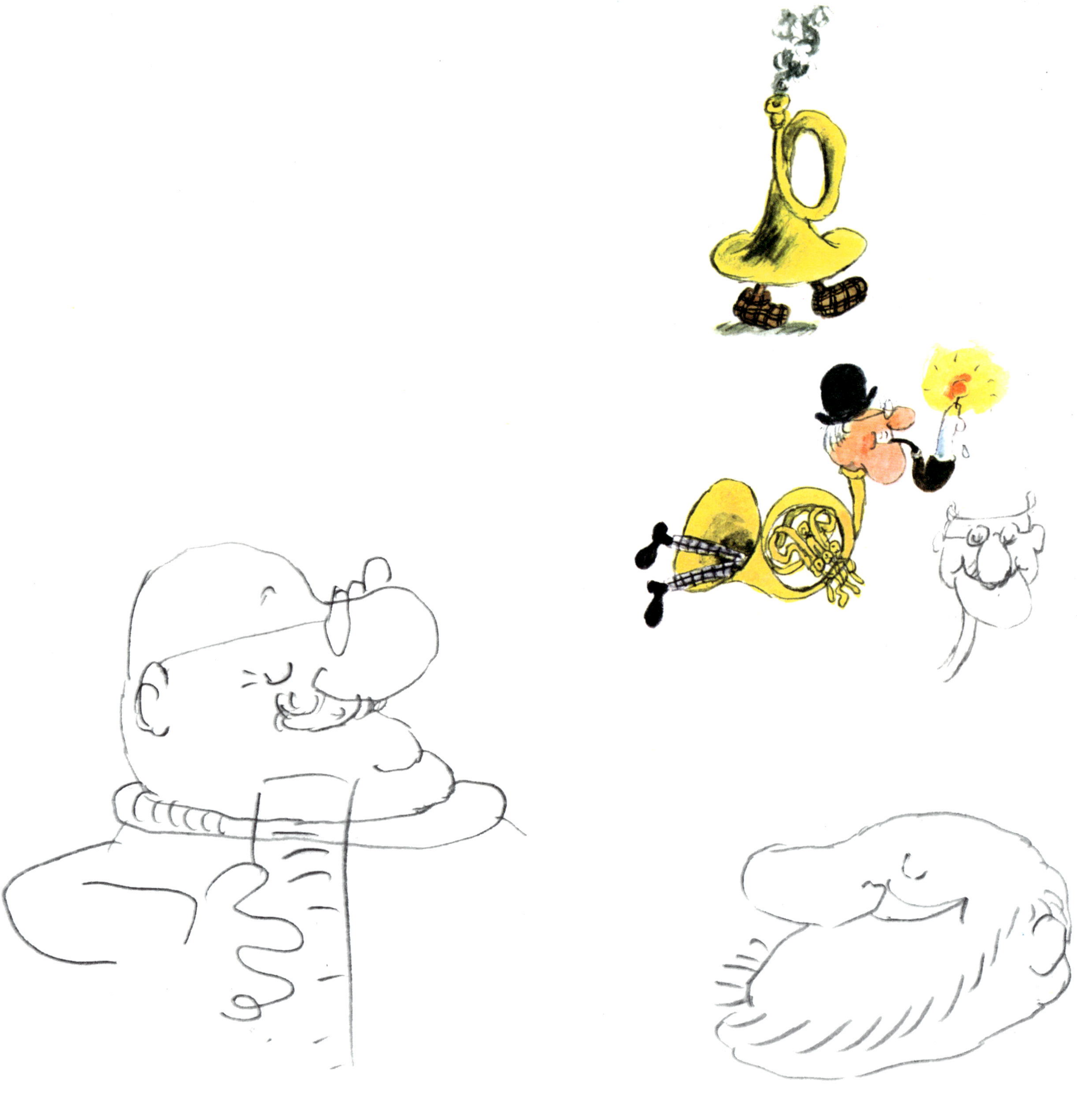

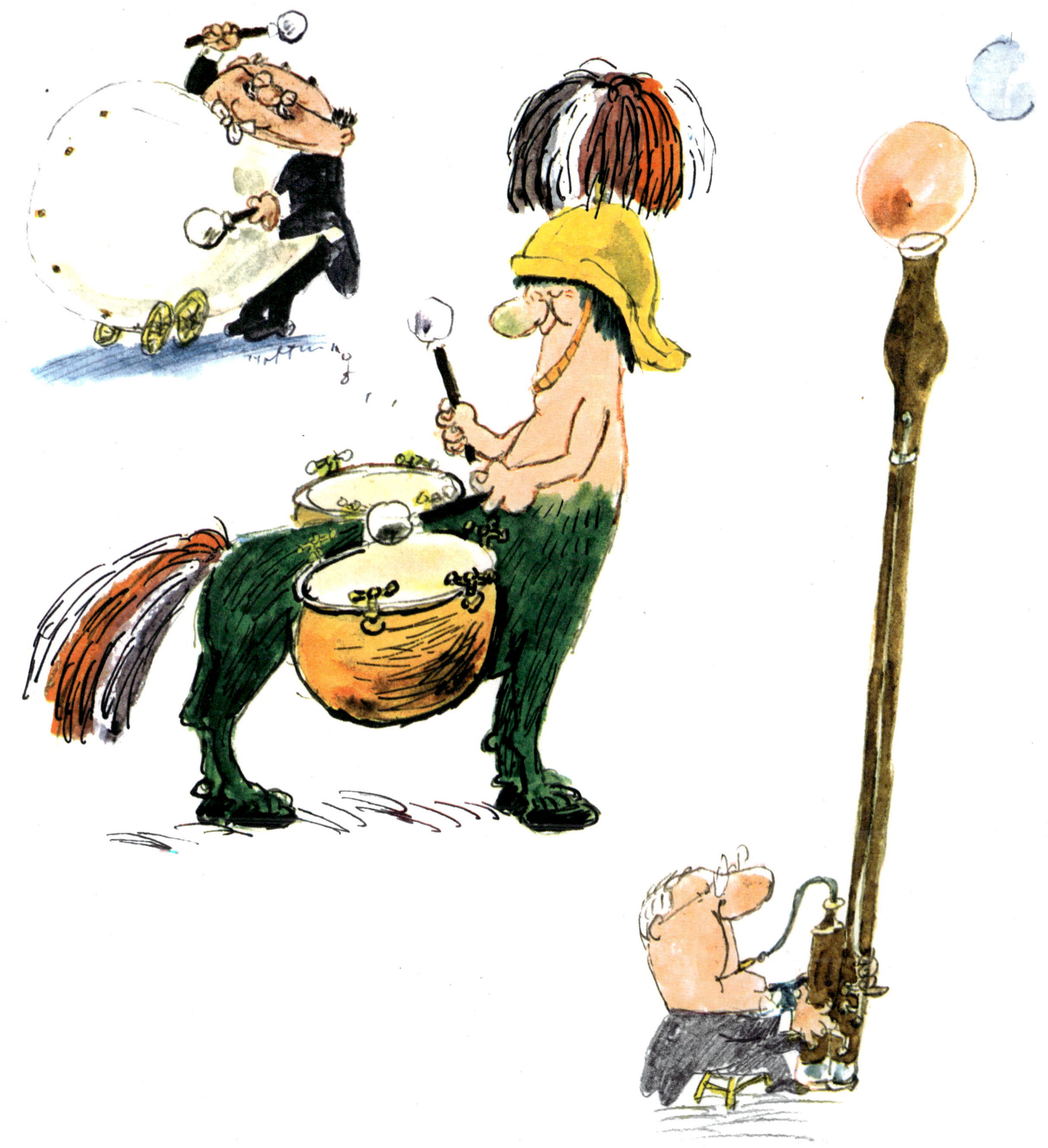

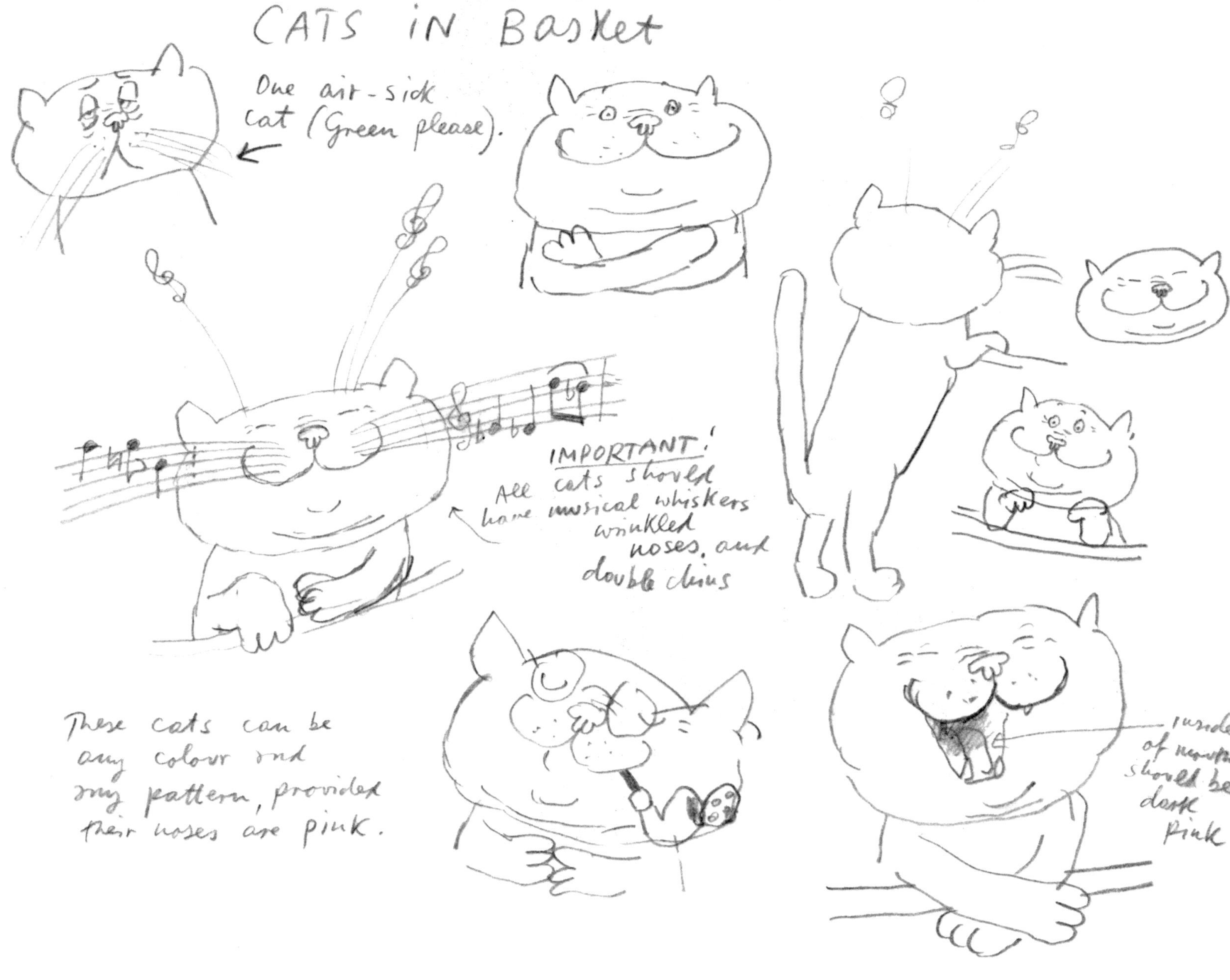
CATS IN Basket
One air-sick cat (Green please).
IMPORTANT! All cats should have musical whiskers wrinkled noses, and double chins
These cats can be any colour and any pattern, provided their noses are pink.
inside of mouth should be dark pink

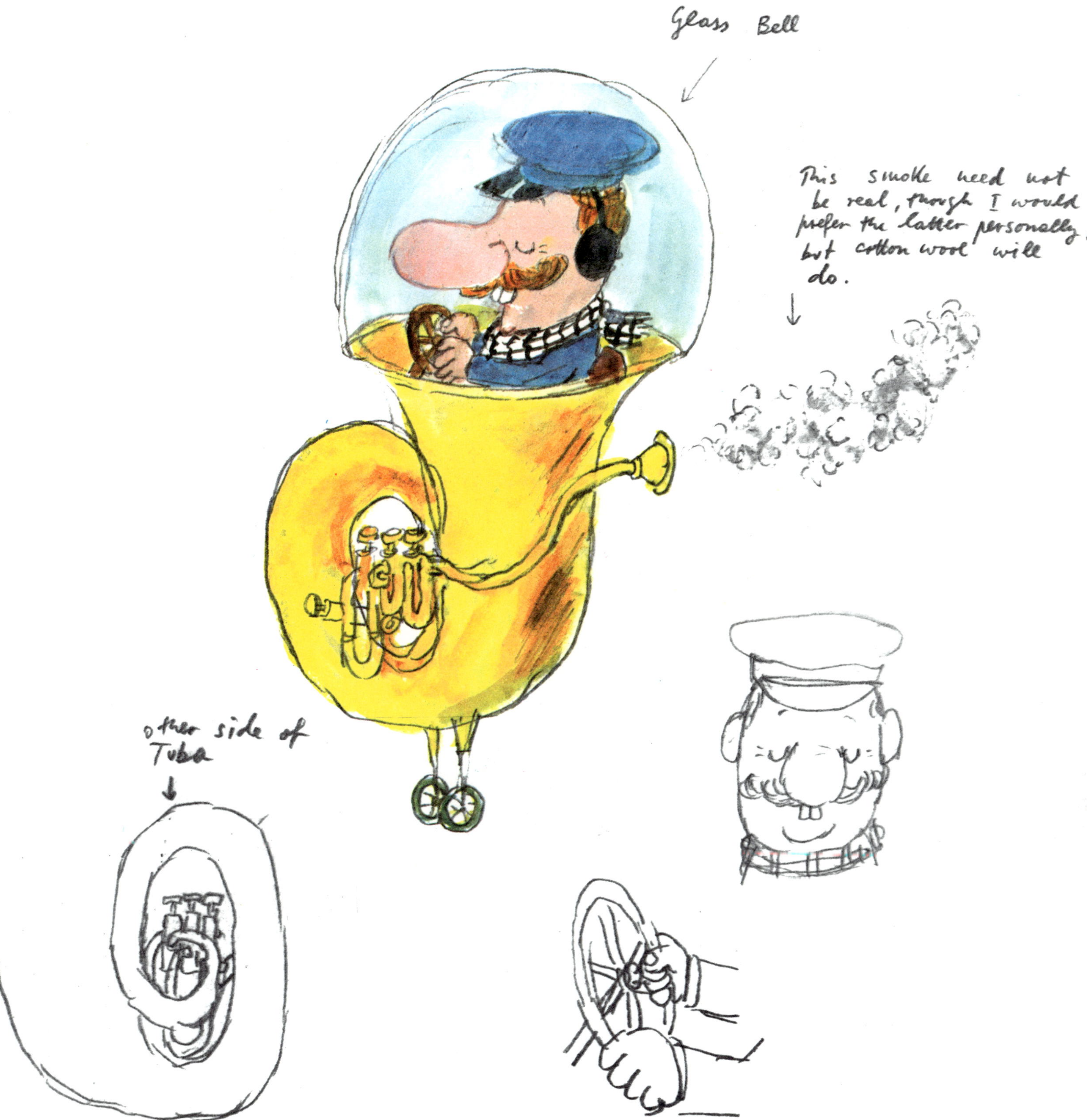
Glass Bell
This smoke need not be real, though I would prefer the latter personally, but cotton wool will do.
other side of Tuba

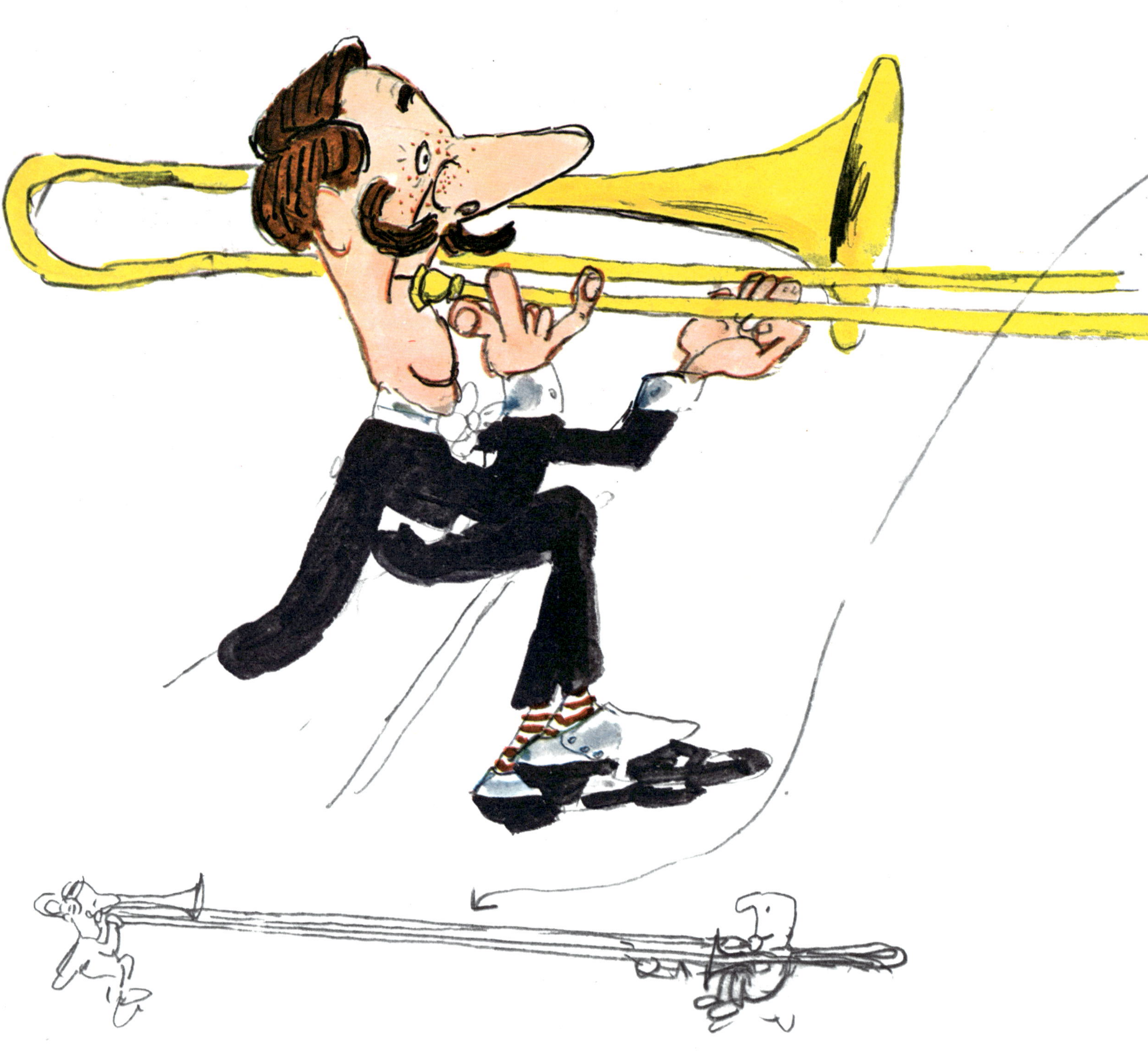

These two Trombones must be joined thus and must stretch from one side of the hall to the other

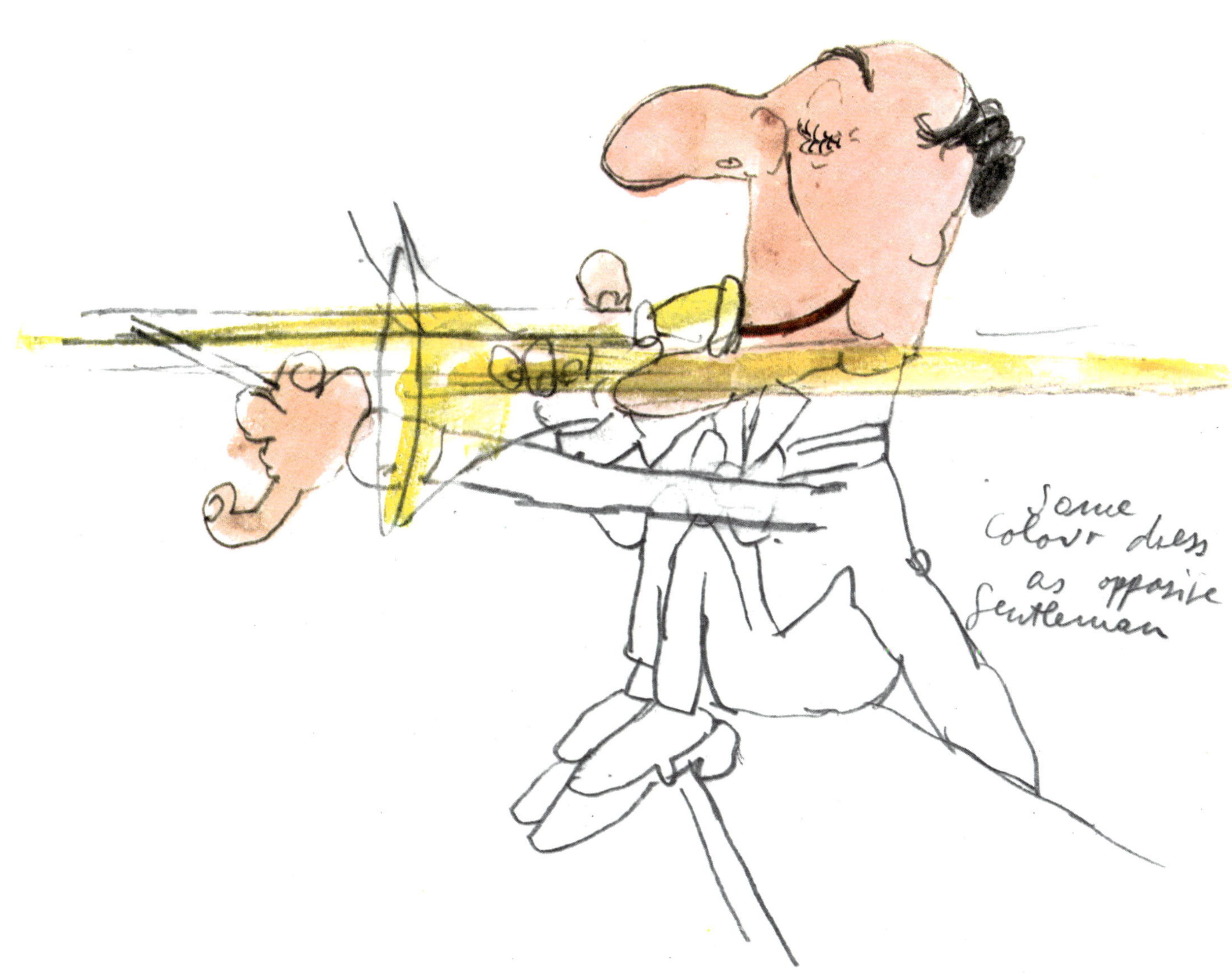

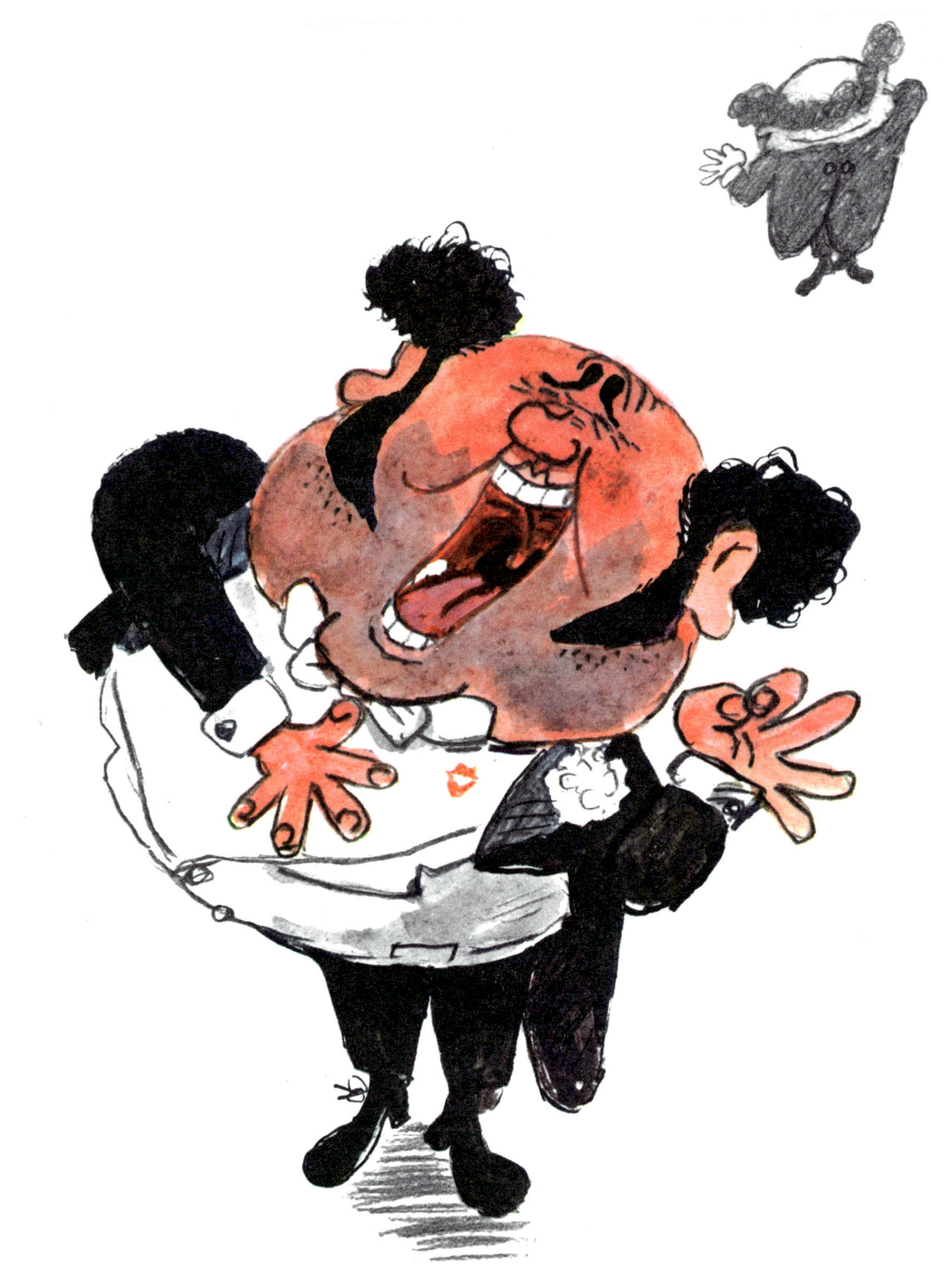

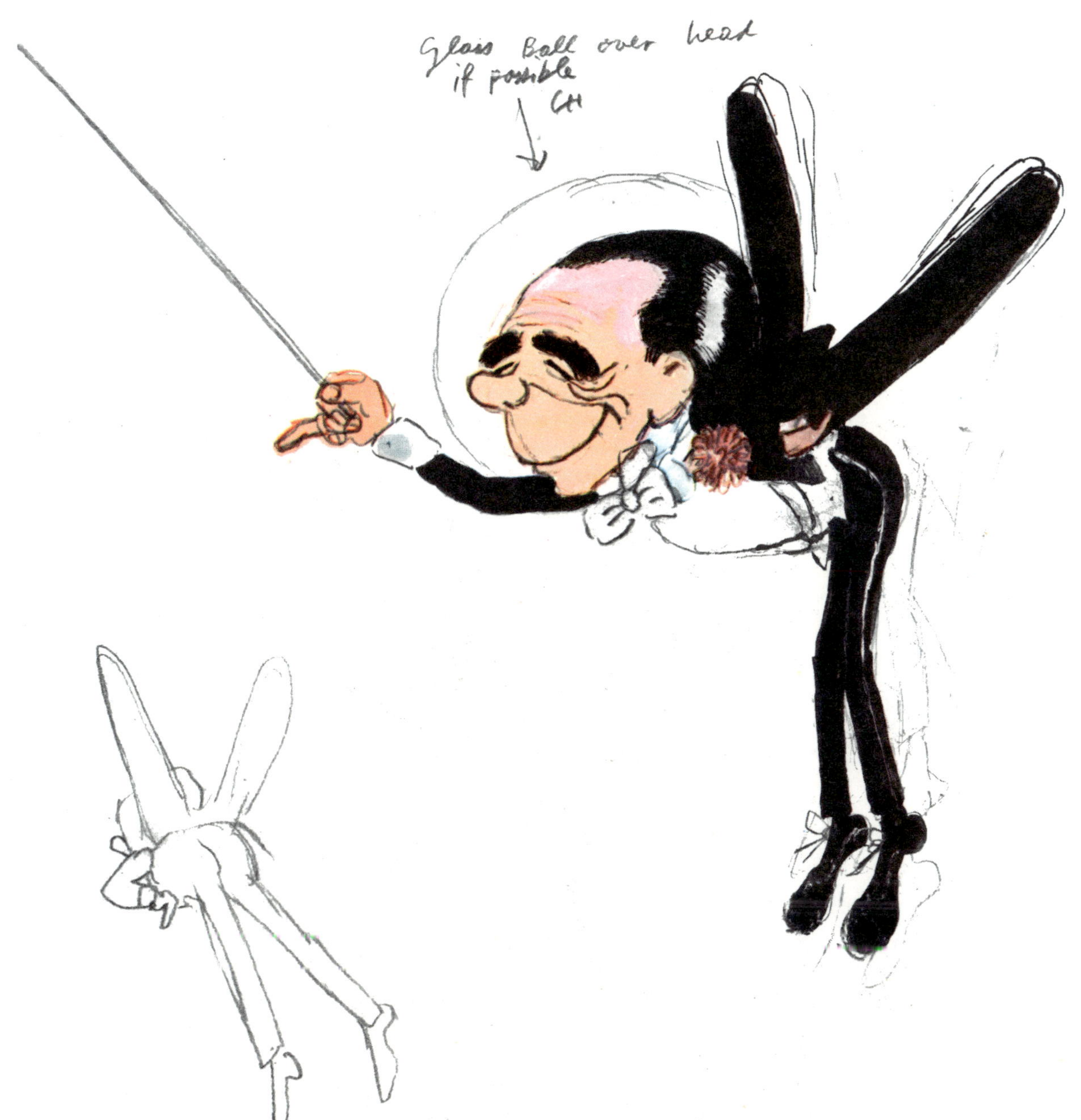
Glass Ball over head
if possible
CH

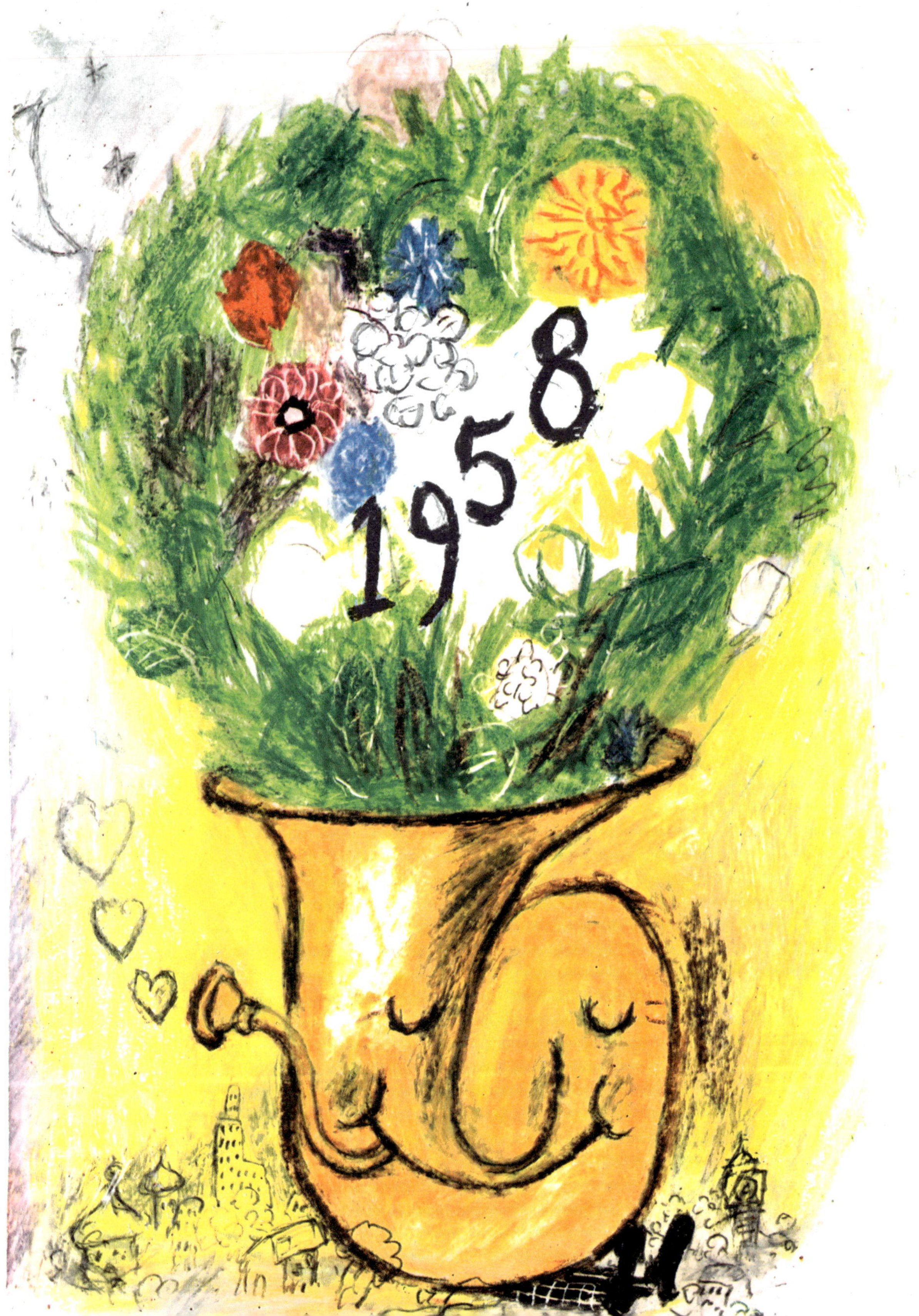
1958

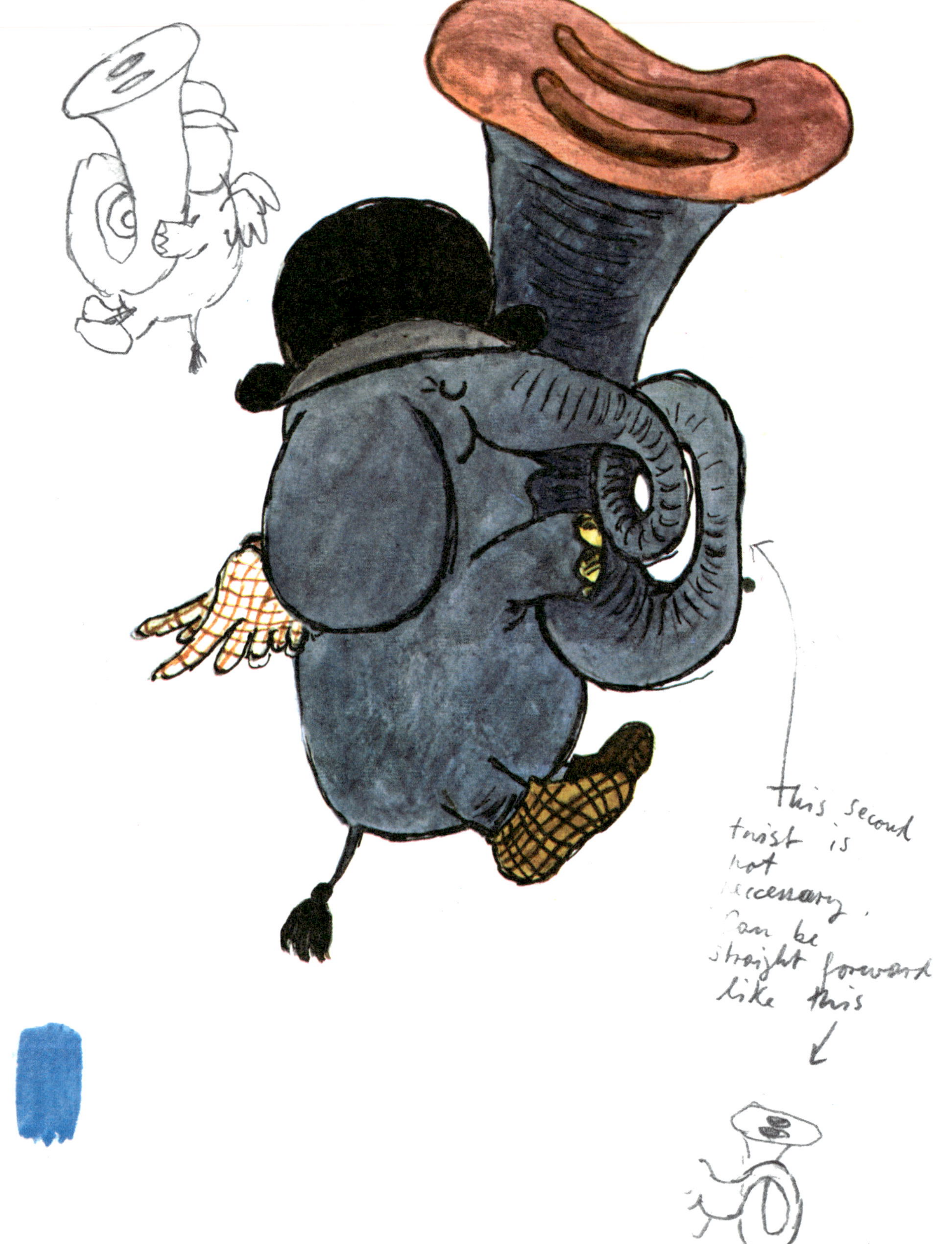
This second twist is not necessary. Can be straight forward like this